Beyond the Paycheck

A Practical Plan to Eliminate Debt, Master Your Money, and Build Wealth on Any Income

Steven Heimlich

To request permission, contact the publisher at BeyondThePaycheck@Consultant.com

ISBN: 979-8-9953008-0-9 (Paperback)

ISBN: 979-8-9953008-1-6 (E-book)

ISBN: 979-8-9953008-2-3 (Audiobook)

First Edition: 2026

Printed in the United States of America.

Acknowledgment and Dedication

To my children, who are the true inspiration for this project. What started as a single page of financial advice has transformed into a full roadmap—partly because I wanted to show you that you can take a simple idea, turn it into a full project, and ultimately guide it to the finish line. I want you to grow up knowing you have the absolute freedom to chase whatever career or passion fulfills you. Learning how to manage your money properly means you'll always have the foundation to live life on your own terms.

Love you.

Contents

Disclaimer and Limitation of Liability

This book is for educational and informational purposes only. **All information is provided on an "as-is" basis, without warranties of any kind, either express or implied, including but not limited to implied warranties of merchantability or fitness for a particular purpose.**

The author is not a certified financial planner, fiduciary, attorney, medical professional, or tax expert. The information in this book is based on the author's personal experience and research and does not constitute personalized financial, legal, or tax advice. Reading this book does not establish a professional advisor-client relationship. You are solely responsible for your financial decisions. Before making any major financial moves, consult a qualified professional to address your specific situation.

The author and publisher assume no liability or responsibility for errors, omissions, or any losses or damages resulting from the use or misuse of this information. **In no event shall the author or publisher's total liability to you for any damages, losses, or causes of action exceed the purchase price of this book.** All trademarks and registered trademarks mentioned are owned by their respective owners.

Investments Risk & Forward-Looking Statements

All investing carries the risk of loss, including losing your original investment. Past performance of the stock market or specific funds does not promise similar results in the future.

Forward-looking statements, mathematical projections, and references to specific securities or portfolio benchmarks (e.g., VOO, FSKAX, NOBL) are provided solely for illustrative purposes and do not serve as specific buy recommendations. Financial data, tax limits, and interest rates reflect 2026 figures and are subject to change.

Peripheral Topics: Strategies for managing mental stress are not a substitute for professional medical or psychological therapy. Any real estate strategies discussed must comply with federal Fair Housing laws and local regulations. References to third-party apps or services are not endorsements of their security or performance; always practice standard digital safety. At publication, the author receives no financial compensation or affiliate commissions for recommending any tools or services mentioned in this book.

Case Studies and Examples: All case studies, profiles, and scenarios included in this book are for illustrative purposes only. Names, details, and exact financial figures have been fictionalized, anonymized, or combined to protect privacy and confidentiality. Any similarity to actual persons, living or deceased, is purely coincidental.

AI Disclosure: Artificial intelligence (AI) tools were used strictly as research and drafting aids. They did not provide financial advice or develop the presented strategies. Despite careful review, rapidly changing markets mean some figures may become outdated or contain errors. The author retains full copyright over the human-authored text, creative arrangement, and core financial methods within this work.

Governing Law: Any disputes, claims, or legal actions related to the information in this book shall be governed by and interpreted according to the laws of the Commonwealth of Massachusetts, without considering its conflict of law principles.

Severability: If any provision of this disclaimer is found to be void, invalid, or unenforceable by a court of competent jurisdiction, that specific provision shall be deemed severed from the rest of the document, and the remaining provisions shall continue in full force and effect.

Introduction

At 29, Kim found herself staring at her bank statement. She had just $87 left and still five days before her next paycheck. Kim wasn't careless. Instead, like 61% of U.S. adults, she was trapped in a paycheck-to-paycheck cycle, with little hope and no roadmap for the economic freedom she desperately wanted.

The U.S. financial system, paired with the pressures of modern social media, can feel crushing, fueled by relentless ads promising easy access to credit and influencers touting the newest "get-rich-quick" scheme. Paid experts are guilting moms into buying the latest "must-have" gadget for their children. Algorithms are so advanced that targeted ads based on what you or someone on the same Wi-Fi searched hours ago lands in your inbox or in-feed banners of your favorite apps with "one-time offers", making spending effortless. The result? Millions in the "middle class" are stuck in an endless spiral of debt. Spend, work, spend some more, repeat.

While finding a windfall can seem like the only way out, the truth is that lasting financial freedom doesn't necessarily have to mean working longer or earning more. Instead, it's about mastering your finances through deliberate, consistent habits.

And Kim proved it. Her first move was to cut down $50 a week on takeout. Combining that with other minor lifestyle changes and a relentless focus on tracking her expenses, she paid off $3,000 in debt and built a $1,500 emergency fund within a year. Now, unlike the more than 75% of American adults who have less than $1,000 in savings, Kim had some cushion. And more importantly, she had momentum and hope. Kim's story demonstrates how one small but smart choice can jumpstart a total rewrite of a financial future.

Knowing my kids would eventually have to navigate the same financial maze, and that school and society leave out many practical lessons for them as they enter the workforce, I knew I had to leave them some guidance. I didn't originally set out to write a personal finance book. I set out to provide a simple guide for my children. What started as a few pointers then led to the 13-step guide—in case I wasn't around to teach them myself. As the guide grew, I realized that other people navigating the same financial maze could benefit from a bit of help. This book is intended to be that map to help guide along the financial maze.

Beyond the Paycheck offers a step-by-step guide to breaking free and building lasting financial security through small but powerful money habits to help compound wealth, whether you are starting with $50 or $50,000. The system comprises three phases: Foundation, Accumulation, and Financial Freedom. The goal is to meet all types of people where they are, helping individuals take back control of their financial destiny by spending decisively, budgeting with clarity, and investing for freedom.

Many modern YouTube financial gurus often promote rigid, one-size-fits-all rules—such as eating nothing but rice and beans to avoid all debt. On the other hand, some traditional financial advisors will base their 'expert' advice on a simpler two-step approach: just build an emergency fund and invest in the stock market. While that's not bad advice per se, it completely overlooks the core challenge of freeing up capital for savings or investment accounts in the first place. Instead of focusing on what to do with money you don't yet have, we begin by building a strong foundation through better, more consistent, and more intentional habits. Because if you don't consistently create new savings to invest in, it won't matter where the stock market is in the next 10, 20, or 30 years.

Most people don't fail to build wealth because they don't earn enough; they fail because they aren't disciplined enough or wait too long to start. None of the concepts or math in this book are revolutionary. Building a solid financial foundation is not about finding some hidden trick; it's about executing proven, math-based systems.

Behavioral Finance studies show that almost 70% of overspending is driven by emotional stress or the dreaded "fear-of-missing-out." But what happens when your long-term goals become the thing you fear missing out on? By aligning spending habits with long-term goals, you can better resist the social traps that suffocate financial flexibility, like so-called "lifestyle creep" where a $4,000 raise can quickly vanish into a fancier car or some niche, influencer-peddled TikTok product. Celebrating small wins and learning from mistakes is the key to the game, and the habits preached in this book will set you up for smart budgeting (Chapter 3) and beyond.

Your Future Is Your Responsibility

It's tempting to wait for a "better time" to save or hope for a government safety net to catch you later. But relying on outside help is a high-risk gamble with your life. Programs like Social Security are under constant pressure, and waiting for a bailout is a plan built on sand. By cutting out financial static, like mindless convenience purchases or a monthly luxury subscription you barely use, you aren't losing out on anything. You are reclaiming your income and using it as leverage for your financial future. Every dollar you invest in your 20s or 30s continues to grow on itself so you don't have to work twice as hard in your 60s and 70s. Taking full control now means that when life gets messy, or the economy shifts, you aren't waiting for a bailout or a check that may never arrive. You've already built your own safety net. You are the ultimate decision-maker for your money and your future. Always do your own due diligence or consult a professional before executing any major financial moves, especially if you aren't completely sure about a specific strategy.

Too Long to Read? Start Here to Break Free

This book cuts through the noise, guiding you toward financial freedom with small, intentional steps. Want a quick start without diving into the full plan? Try these today and build confidence as you explore the deeper chapters.

1. Track Your Spending: Use a notebook, an Excel sheet, or an app like Empower to review your expenses from last month and see exactly where your paycheck goes and how your finances stand. Cancel any unused or unnecessary subscriptions immediately.

2. Start Automating: Arrange autopayments for essential bills and make a small weekly transfer (e.g., $25) to a high-yield savings account to gain momentum. See Chapter 4 for a complete automation plan.

3. Tackle High-Interest Debt: Use the avalanche or snowball strategies (Chapter 7) to conquer loans and credit card debt. Prioritize paying off any debt above 6% as aggressively as possible while maintaining minimum payments on the others.

These simple habits generate momentum and support the idea that you must protect first before you grow. Start Chapter 1 now and let the full system guide you to financial freedom.

CHAPTER 1

Mental Health and Money: Taming Financial Stress

It's 2 a.m. You're awake with your heart pounding as if you've just run a marathon. The $150 electric bill you forgot about is now tormenting you. Your mind starts to spiral: How will I pay for this? Do I need to get another job? If you find yourself feeling this way, you're not alone. According to the American Psychological Association, 65% of Americans report financial stress as a major mental health burden. Money worries can feel overwhelming, but you have the tools to overcome that anxiety. It's okay to feel stressed because money can be emotional. But the sooner you take small, intentional steps to get your finances in order, the quicker you'll reduce the stress and steer your finances toward calmer waters. Turn the panic into confidence with practical habits that anyone can do that will put both your mind and your wallet at ease.

Why Mental Health and Money Matter

Money isn't just strictly about numbers; it's tied to your anxiety and that knot in your stomach when a surprise car repair bill hits. Financial stress can drain all of your energy and even strain relationships. Every step you take, whether it's saving $80 that you'd normally spend during a weekend or cutting a $10 unnecessary daily habit, builds a bridge towards better peace of mind. You're not aiming for perfection at this point; you're aiming for progress.

How to Tame Financial Stress

1. Start Tiny, Win Big

Overwhelmed? That's normal. Start by tracking a single day's spending or setting a $20-per-week auto-transfer to a high-yield savings account (HYSA). Banking institutions like Capital One offer competitive rates—often 10x higher than traditional brick-and-mortar banks. Saving $20 per week adds up to over $1,000 a year, usually enough for a small emergency. Each win chips away at the anxiety. The small actions will compound into confidence, and that confidence will eventually kill the anxiety.

2. Breathe Through the Budget

Budgeting sounds frustrating and tedious, but it's your remedy for financial stress. Try the 60/20/20 budget from Chapter 3: 60% for Essentials (rent, groceries, utility bills), 20% for Savings and Investing (HYSA, 401k, debt payoff), and 20% for Personal Spending (takeout, movies, Netflix). Use an app like Simplifi or Empower to track spending for 30 days. If apps aren't your style, jot down expenses in a notebook or on an Excel sheet. Redirecting just $50 each month to savings helps cut stress and builds a $600 cushion within one year.

3. Lean on Available Resources

Call 211 or visit the National Foundation for Credit Counseling (NFCC.org) for free advice and financial counseling in your area. Think of these resources as having a free money coach in your back pocket, available anytime you need them. Join Reddit's r/personalfinance or similar subreddit communities for tips from folks who've been there (and survived).

Don't ignore anxiety that finances can trigger. If you feel overwhelmed, try trusted apps like Calm or Headspace that offer quick guided sessions, which can help you reset and breathe easier. These tools help ease your mind and help you focus on what you can control.

4. Share the Weight

Money stress loves isolation. Talk to a trusted friend, partner, or family member about one financial goal, like "I want to save $1,000 this year for a golf weekend." Sharing makes it real and keeps you accountable. Or join a local money meetup (check Meetup.com) to swap tips over coffee. Connection turns stress into teamwork.

Case Study: Erik's Stress-to-Success Story

Erik, 23, a pharmacy tech earning $41,000, used to lose sleep over his $3,500 credit card debt. The 24% interest felt like a ticking time bomb. Overwhelmed? Absolutely. But he started small: he used Empower to track spending, cutting $60 per week on takeout, saving over $200 a month. He automated $80 per month to a SoFi HYSA to build a starter emergency fund, hitting $960 in a year. When a $450 car repair hit, he paid in cash to avoid more debt. "I went from panic to power," Erik said, now sleeping like a baby. He reads one r/personalfinance thread on Reddit daily and shares tips with coworkers.

Erik turned sleepless nights into a $960 safety net in a year, proving small moves can silence big worries. The sooner you start, the sooner your finances feel like a trusted tool.

CHAPTER 2

Live Below Your Means

You cannot out-earn a bad spending habit. Whether you earn $40,000 or $400,000, the key concept of financial freedom is the same: **wealth is about spending less than you earn**. Spending $50 a week on office cafe lunches can add up to $2,600 a year, and a few expensive after-work cocktails with your co-workers can add up just as fast. **High income does not equal wealth.** If you bring home $10,000 a month, spending the full $10,000 a month keeps your wealth at exactly zero. The proper way to determine true wealth is by calculating your net worth, which is simply the total value of everything you own minus everything you owe. If your paycheck grows but your net worth stays stagnant, the main culprit for this is lifestyle creep.

Lifestyle creep is when your expenses continue to grow as your income increases. It doesn't always appear through flashy purchases or expensive vacations; often, it sneaks in with a slightly bigger apartment, a new car payment, or a bunch of monthly subscriptions you forget about. By mastering goal-oriented spending and resisting the urge to inflate your lifestyle, you'll be able to direct money toward what truly matters, like becoming debt-free or building towards a secure retirement.

How to Spend Smart and Stay Steady

Align Spending with Goals

Before making any purchase, ask yourself: Does this get me closer to my goals or further away from them? That $150 on a new pair of sneakers might feel like a win today, but putting the same money toward high-yield savings or crushing high-interest debt moves you closer to your goals. Keep things that add value to you, like your daily coffee if it lifts your mood each morning, but cut out what doesn't. According to recent data, the average person wastes over $200 a year on unused subscriptions. That's money that could be better used for something that actually matters to you.

Save the First Dollar, Not the Last Dollar

Don't wait to see what's left over at the end of the month. Decide your savings target first—the 'first dollar'—and build your lifestyle around whatever remains. If you wait to save whatever is left over, you will inevitably save nothing. **By paying yourself first, you force your lifestyle to adapt to the remaining budget.**

Resist Lifestyle Creep

When you get a raise, the temptation to upgrade everything is typically a trap. If you earn a $2,500 pay increase, hold off on changing your budget right away. Let a month or two of those larger paychecks land in your bank account before adjusting your spending. The reality is that most Americans never increase their savings rate after receiving a raise. Instead, they trade their long-term financial security for immediate, fleeting gratification.

Review your numbers and stay consistent. Every dollar moved into your HYSA or retirement account puts you ahead of 60% of the country.

Track Every Dollar

Tracking every dollar isn't a chore; as discussed in Chapter 1, it instead helps reduce stress. For 30 days, track where every dollar goes. Awareness is the first step to change, and the first step to silencing financial anxiety. You'll be shocked at what you find. The average American spends over $275 a month on impulse buys— purchases they didn't plan for, and usually regret. That adds up to more than $3,300 a year that could have gone towards an emergency fund or a bucket-list trip.

Pause Impulse Buys

If it costs over $100 and isn't essential, give yourself 24 hours before buying. That $200 concert ticket might sound amazing right now, but if it sets back your emergency fund, you'll feel it later. In a recent survey, over 60% of people who used a 24-hour rule said it helped them avoid regrets and prioritize bigger goals. Make space between impulse and action. You'll thank yourself later.

Avoid Buy Now, Pay Later Traps

Services like Klarna and Affirm make big purchases seem affordable with "easy" installments, but they can be a sneaky way to overspend. A $400 gadget split into four payments might feel painless today, but stacking multiple plans creates a snowball of debt that hits your bank account all at once. Then if you miss a payment you're slammed with late fees and credit score damage that can linger for years. Skip the BNPL illusion. A high percentage of BNPL users reported credit damage from missed payments, according to the Consumer Financial Protection Bureau. If you can't pay cash today, you can't afford it. Save up instead to keep your spending in check and your credit strong.

FOMO Spending

Social media, especially TikTok, is designed to make you spend more. In 2025 alone, users spent over $15.8 billion through TikTok Shop, and more than 70% bought something after seeing it in their feed or stories. That's not just a coincidence; it's a deliberate impulse. Do not fall for influencer "master classes" promising some shortcut to riches. Fight back by curating your feed. Follow creators who focus on building wealth (#MoneyMindset, #DebtFreeJourney), not just spending it. Then set a limit on your "trend" spending at $75 per month (or whatever fits your budget) with a budgeting app like Simplifi or YNAB. You can still enjoy yourself while staying in control.

The Mobile Gambling and 'Social Casino' Trap

Sports betting and "social casinos" are no longer restricted to a special weekend in Vegas or Atlantic City. The action is constantly sitting in your pocket, even sending push notifications not to miss the next big game or slots promo. Mobile sportsbooks lure people in with "risk-free" promos, making it dangerously easy to throw $100 on a Sunday football parlay you never intended to originally place. But make no mistake: this isn't investing, and you don't have an edge. These gambling apps use advanced algorithms designed to ensure the house wins over time, just like in Vegas. Even more deceptive are "social casinos"—apps with cartoon graphics that bypass traditional gambling laws by having you buy "gold coins" or "sweeps coins." These are specifically engineered to trigger the same dopamine loops as a physical slot machine, quietly draining your bank account through quick $5 or $10 transactions.

Stop Chasing Losses

The most dangerous phase of gambling isn't the first bet; it's what happens after you lose. The psychological urge to "win back" your money and the endless pursuit of that dopamine high lead directly to chasing losses. What may start as a $100 loss quickly turns into a panicked $200 bet, and suddenly, you are pulling from your grocery money or swiping a high-interest credit card to cover the gap. This vicious cycle is exactly how casual entertainment can spiral into crippling debt and severe addiction. According to the National Council on Problem Gambling, gambling addiction has surged in direct correlation with the expansion of mobile gambling legislation across the United States over the past several years. Treat gambling as an occasional hobby that is used for entertainment only and done only with money you can afford to lose.

Name Your Goals

Give your money a purpose. Rename your savings accounts to things like "Home Fund," "Friends Vacation", "Guitar Lesson", or "New Car." It almost sounds too simple, but it works. In fact, research shows people who label savings accounts are significantly more likely to reach their goals. Purposeful spending transforms your money into a tool for your dreams. Start today. You're closer to financial freedom than you think!

Action Steps

- **Define one financial goal (e.g., debt freedom, emergency fund).**
- **Track all expenses for 30 days using a budgeting app or a spreadsheet.**
- **Apply the 24-hour rule to one non-essential purchase this week.**
- **Cut one small expense (e.g., a $15 per month subscription) and redirect to a named "Vacation Fund."**

CHAPTER 3

Budgeting Your Way

A budget does not have to be a financial restriction; it's meant as a tool that aligns your spending with your true necessities. Whether you are aggressively paying off debt or building up your savings and retirement, a budget puts you in full control. This chapter introduces two effective budgeting methods—60/20/20 and Zero-Based Budgeting (ZBB)—and helps you choose the one that best fits your life. By the end, you'll have clear steps to start budgeting today.

Why Budgeting Matters

Without a budget, money easily escapes your control. As we saw in Chapter 2, those impulsive purchases add up quickly and are often triggered by social media ads. A budget helps you curb emotional spending and focus on what matters, whether it's a $2,000 emergency fund or a $5,000 investment. Think of it as a plan to make your money work just as hard as you do. Once you know where your money is going each month, it is that much easier to plug the leaks draining your wealth.

Budgeting Frameworks

60/20/20 Budget

This framework divides your after-tax income into three categories:

- **60% Essentials:** Absolute necessities like rent, utilities, groceries, and minimum monthly debt payments.
- **20% Savings and Investing:** Emergency fund, investments, or additional debt payments.
- **20% Personal Spending:** Fun stuff. Dining out, hobbies, travel, subscriptions, or events.

Example: If you earn $4,000 per month after taxes, that's $2,400 for essential needs, $800 for savings, investing, or debt relief, and $800 for personal discretionary spending. It's simple and flexible, ideal for beginners or those who want a low-maintenance plan.

Zero-Based Budgeting (ZBB)

ZBB assigns every dollar a specific purpose before the month starts. Your income minus your planned expenses must total exactly zero. You categorize all spending (for example, $1,200 for rent, $300 for groceries, $50 for dining out), but savings and debt payments are not 'leftovers'; they are deliberate line items. If you end up with $200 unallocated, you immediately assign it: $100 to debt, $100 to savings. It's detailed and hands-on, ideal for those seeking total control or with irregular income.

Example: With $4,000 per month, you'd plan every dollar, allocating $1,500 to rent, $400 to groceries, $375 to your car, $150 to utilities, $75 to subscriptions, $500 to debt, $1,000 to savings, until every single dollar is assigned and your balance is zero.

Choosing Your Framework

The 60/20/20 budget fits those who want simplicity and flexibility, such as busy professionals or newcomers to budgeting. Usually, it works best for middle-income earners (e.g., $45,000 to $75,000 in lower-cost-of-living areas or $75,000 to $100,000 in higher-cost-of-living areas). ZBB, however, is better for detail-oriented people, those with variable income, or anyone managing high debt. Try different numbers with your own paycheck and monthly bills to find what works for you.

The 60/20/20 framework can be adjusted based on your income and cost of living. Lower-income earners should favor a 70/15/15 breakdown, while higher-income earners should lean toward a 50/30/20 breakdown.

If you have a lower salary in a high-cost-of-living metro area, consider the 75/15/10 breakdown. This recognizes that your area is expensive while maintaining the core of your financial habits. Once you receive a promotion or a raise, you can shift to a 70/15/15 budget. While this temporary adjustment slightly exceeds the 33% housing guardrail discussed later in Chapter 9, it reflects the tough reality of living on entry-level wages in costly zip codes. There is no shame in this stage of life. Make this short-term adjustment to survive now, with the clear goal of reducing your essentials ratio and increasing your investing and savings ratio as your income increases.

Getting Started

1. **Pick a Framework:** Using the spending data you started tracking in Chapter 2, choose either the 60/20/20 method for simplicity or ZBB for precision. Test either one out for 30 days.

2. **Adjust and Commit:** Review weekly. If you're overspending on wants, consider cutting one subscription (e.g., pausing an unused gym membership, removing an unused music service, or downgrading a premium software program).

Budgeting is not about getting it perfectly right on the first try. Pick a framework today, map out your next paycheck, and take control of your financial life.

CHAPTER 4

Comprehensive Automation - Your Financial Autopilot

Ever missed paying a bill because life got too busy, or paid a pointless $35 late fee for forgetting to transfer money from one account to another? Human willpower is limited. Automation removes the need for willpower altogether. By setting your finances on autopilot, you ensure that your monthly bills and wealth-building goals are handled—effortlessly, every paycheck. With distractions everywhere today, automating your bills, savings, investments, and any major purchases makes sure your money works for you. From monthly utility bills to retirement saving, this system helps you succeed without the stress.

Why Automation Works

Manual saving, investing, and bill paying require discipline and attentiveness that can be hard to maintain when life gets busy. Automation eliminates decision fatigue, ensuring consistency. By automatically investing $100 per month in an index fund (with assumed growth of 7% per year), you can save roughly $121,000 within 30 years, without lifting a finger after setup. It's like setting a GPS: choose your destination and let it guide you. A recent survey found that 65% of users who automated savings felt more confident in their finances.

Automation is the most reliable way to overcome your own human psychology. If you haven't set up your direct deposit to automatically split a portion into a High-Yield Savings Account (HYSA) for your emergency fund, you're not following the system. Stop relying solely on willpower to manage your money and let automation handle the heavy lifting. Automation turns financial discipline into a hands-off process.

How to Automate Your Finances

Savings for Emergencies and Goals

Direct 10% of your paycheck to a high-yield savings account (HYSA) with a competitive interest rate. Build the HYSA up to one month of essentials for your starter emergency fund. This account is meant for unexpected, unpredictable expenses, such as medical bills, car repairs, and home repairs. Being able to tap into this account for unexpected bills lets you avoid putting the expense on a credit card and avoid further debt.

Investments for Wealth

Many successful investors set up bi-weekly or monthly transfers of $100+ to a Roth IRA, 401(k), or brokerage account with a trusted investing company such as Vanguard or Fidelity, and choose popular, low-cost ETFs, such as VTI (0.03% fee). Dollar-cost averaging buys more shares when prices dip, smoothing market swings. If you can save 10-15% of your income into retirement, DO IT! As we will cover in Chapter 8, it is highly recommended to automate enough to get your full employer 401(k) match, then bump your automated contribution up by 1% with every annual raise.

Bills for Reliability

Auto-pay rent, utilities, and credit cards to avoid late fees and protect your credit. Set monthly phone or email alerts to review statements for errors or overcharges.

Sinking Funds for Irregular Yearly Purchases

Sinking Funds are for irregular but predictable purchases. Figure out your expected yearly costs (such as a Prime subscription, holiday gifts, birthday gifts, and car excise tax), divide that total by 52, and automate that amount each week to a targeted HYSA. For a $1,000 sinking fund, divide by 52 weeks ($19.23), and round up to a clean $20 per week.

Micro-Investing for Growth

Use apps like Acorns to round up purchases (e.g., $4.25 coffee rounds to $5, investing $0.75). A daily $0.75 round-up adds more than $270/year to your investing portfolio without even including interest gains.

Next-Level Techniques

Split Paychecks

If you are completely debt-free (excluding your mortgage) or free from high-interest loans, direct 50% of raises or bonuses to investments. But don't do it manually. If you automate it to hit right when you receive your next paycheck, you take lifestyle creep right out of the equation. This is discussed in greater detail in Chapter 12.

Tax-Advantaged Accounts

These are accounts that save you taxes. Automate a set amount, such as $80 per month, to an HSA ($4,400 limit, 2026). If you are 55+, you can add an extra $1,000 to an income-tax-free medical savings account or a Traditional IRA catch-up for 50+ years old. **Note: A** High-Deductible Health Plan (HDHP) is necessary here, as this is a critical barrier to entry. HDHPs are discussed in greater detail in Chapter 10.

Case Study: Kiera's Rise

Kiera, 30, an HR specialist earning $71,000, struggled to save consistently. She automated her finances: $200 a month to a SoFi HYSA (4% APY) for emergencies, $160 to a Vanguard Roth IRA (VTI ETF) for retirement, $500 per month for bills to avoid late fees, and $60 per month to a 'Laptop and Phone Fund' HYSA. In three years, she saved $7,200, invested more than $5,700, and paid cash for a new laptop, avoiding debt. She now reviews her automations annually to find new ways to boost contributions.

Action Steps

- Set up an auto-draft to your HYSA or retirement account today. It completely removes your willpower from the equation.
- Automate your minimum credit card payments today to avoid late fees.
- Automate one savings goal in the next ten minutes. Small, consistent moves are the most proven path to a future of ease.

CHAPTER 5

Emergency Funds

It's midnight, you're about to head home, and your car won't start. The tow truck costs $200, plus whatever the mechanic deems the fix to be the next day and payday is still five days away. Without an emergency fund in place, this potential $1,000 (or more) surprise becomes a financial disaster that forces you to use a high-interest credit card to cover the cost. But if you had a safety net in place it would be just a minor inconvenience. An emergency fund acts as your financial firewall, preventing a temporary financial crisis from turning into compounding debt.

Why It Matters

Being broke can be expensive. When you don’t have cash on hand, life charges you a premium to solve these problems by using a credit card or high-interest loans.

Consider the math: If you put a $1,000 emergency on a credit card with 22% interest and make only minimum payments, you aren’t just paying back $1,000. You are paying back hundreds more in interest over months or years. That new monthly payment eats into your cash flow, making it even harder to save for the next emergency. This is the cycle that keeps people trapped.

If you successfully complete Phase 1 (a 1-month emergency fund), you are already ahead of the 75% of Americans who don't have $1,000 cash available. By the time you reach Phase 2, you will be in the elite 45% of adults who can comfortably survive a three-month job loss, and among the 27% of adults who can survive a six-month job loss.

What Counts as an Emergency?

One of the biggest mistakes people make is raiding this fund for "unexpected" costs that were actually predictable. To protect your funds, you need strict rules in place.

The 3-Question Litmus Test

Before you transfer a single dollar out of your emergency fund HYSA account, ask yourself:

- **Is it unexpected?** Christmas happens every December; that is a predictable expense, not an emergency. A blown transmission is unexpected.
- **Is it necessary?** You *need* a working furnace in January; you *want* a new laptop just because your current one is running slowly.
- **Is it urgent?** Can this wait until next month or your next paycheck, or will delaying payment cause immediate financial or physical harm?

If the answer to all three isn't a resounding 'Yes,' do not touch the fund.

How to Build Your Safety Net

Building this fund can feel daunting, especially if things are tight. Do not try to do it all at once. Break it down into two distinct phases.

Phase 1: The Starter Fund (1 Month of Essentials)

Your immediate priority is to save one full month of essential living expenses. This is your immediate outlet if something unexpected comes up— such as, flat tires, pet vet bills, minor home repairs—so you don't have to reach for a credit card.

- **Calculate your 'lean survival number'** by adding up strictly what you need to stay alive and employed: Rent or Mortgage, Utilities, Basic Groceries (zero dining out), Insurance, Transportation, and Minimum Debt Payments. If that bare-bones number is $3,000, then $3,000 is your Phase 1 goal. You should save as aggressively as possible to reach this goal.

Phase 2: The Fully Funded Security (3–6 Months)

Once you have paid off your high-interest bad debts (like credit cards), you will come back and expand this fund to cover 3 to 6 months of essential living expenses.

- Why so much? This isn't just for a car repair at this point. This is for job loss or medical inability to work. In a volatile economy, it often takes 3 to 6 months to find a new job that matches your previous income. This fund buys you the time to find the right job, not just the first job. Reaching 3 months' worth of essentials is the goal to officially be successful with Phase 2, but 6 months' worth is the ideal goal.

Where to Put the Money

Do not leave this money in your checking account, where it is too easy to spend on a "bad week." Conversely, do not lock it up in investments or CDs where you can't get to it instantly.

A High-Yield Savings Account (HYSA) is your answer. Park these funds in a High-Yield Savings Account with a separate bank from your daily checking (e.g., Ally, Capital One, SoFi, Marcus, etc). Here is why a HYSA is non-negotiable:

- **Out of Sight, Out of Mind:** If you don't see the balance every time you log in to check your regular checking balance, you won't touch it.
- **Fight Inflation:** Because this money will sit untouched for a long time, capitalizing on that higher APY is crucial to fight inflation.
- **Liquidity:** You can transfer the money back to your checking account, usually within 1–2 business days.

The Golden Rule of the Emergency Fund

This money is not an investment. It is insurance. It is not supposed to make you rich; it is supposed to keep you safe.

Split Strategy

Once your Phase 1 Starter Emergency Fund (1 month of essentials) is fully funded, and you have officially paid off all your high-interest consumer debt (like credit cards and personal loans), you might wonder if you should pause your retirement contributions altogether to aggressively build up your safety net towards 3-6 months' worth of essential costs.

The answer is usually no. Instead, use the **Split Strategy**. If your budget allows you to save 12% of your pay each paycheck, split it equally: automate 6% toward your retirement accounts to capture any employer match and keep your market exposure, and put the remaining 6% straight into your high-yield emergency savings account. This balanced approach ensures you're actively building your immediate financial safety net without sacrificing the long-term, compound growth of your investments, since total time in the market is your greatest asset with retirement wealth building. (Note: If you still have high-interest debt, pause after Phase 1 of your emergency fund is funded and throw every extra dollar at the high-interest debt until it is gone, as outlined in Chapter 7).

CHAPTER 6

Protecting Your Wealth (Insurance, Wills, Umbrella, etc.)

You've worked too hard to risk losing all your hard-earned money from one bad day. Insurance premiums are essential to protect your financial progress from being wiped out. Insurance provides you with the ultimate luxury: the ability to recover from a crisis without facing financial ruin. With medical and repair costs increasing, this chapter shows you how to choose smart coverage without overpaying, whether you're brand new to this or trying to improve an existing plan.

Why Insurance Matters

A single setback, like a $5,000 hospital bill, can wipe out years' worth of savings. If paid with a credit card at a 24% interest rate, that bill incurs $1,200 in interest costs each year until repaid. Smart coverage saves thousands while keeping your goals on track.

Core Insurance Needs

Health

Consider choosing a High-Deductible Health Plan (HDHP) with an HSA to save on taxes. Contribute up to $4,400 (single, 2026) for deductible contributions, tax-free growth, and tax-free medical withdrawals. This saves $968 yearly in the 22% bracket.

Auto

Get liability coverage (required in most states) for damage you cause. Add comprehensive and collision for cars worth over $5,000 to cover repairs.

Homeowners/Renters

If you own a home, homeowners' insurance covers the dwelling and provides liability protection, and your mortgage lender will require it. **If you rent, renters' insurance is optional but should be considered non-negotiable.** It's cheap (often around $20-$25 per month) and covers your belongings against theft, fire, or water damage, and provides liability if someone is injured in your apartment. Landlords only cover the building structure, not your stuff.

Term Life Insurance

If you have dependents, aim for 12-15 times your annual income (e.g., ~$1 million coverage for a $75,000 salary). In 2026, for a healthy, non-smoker 30-year-old, a 20-year Term Life plan costs approximately $45 per month for $1 million of coverage, unlike the more expensive whole life option. Everyone's situation is different, so it is important to weigh options based on your specific profile, e.g., whether you have kids and how much other debt you carry. Use a term life insurance calculator to get a

more precise number for your specific family's needs. While many experts consider 10x your annual salary to be the standard baseline, aiming for 12–15x is typically a higher-impact strategy. This "aggressive" multiplier creates a more solid safety net, often ensuring your family isn't just getting by, but has a surplus to cover most of their costs with rising inflation. Get quotes from trusted sources such as PolicyGenius, AAA, or Ethos.

Beneficiaries on All Accounts

It is highly recommended to log in and designate a specific beneficiary for every single bank account, investment account, and life insurance policy you own. Doing this allows these assets to bypass the probate courts entirely.

- **Crucial Warning:** Account-level beneficiaries legally override your Will. If your Will states that all your assets go to your current spouse, but you forgot to remove your ex-spouse as the beneficiary on your 401(k), the bank will legally hand the money to your ex-spouse. Try to check these designations annually.

- **ADDITIONAL NOTE:** If you are married and live in a Community Property state (e.g., California, Texas, Arizona), state law may dictate that your spouse is the primary beneficiary of certain accounts regardless of who you name, unless they sign a waiver. Check your specific state laws to ensure your designations are valid.

Will & Health Proxy

A will outlines how your assets are distributed and who will care for your children, property, and pets. At the same time, a healthcare proxy assigns someone to make medical decisions on your behalf if you're incapacitated.

These documents are essential once you have children, a partner, own a home, or possess meaningful assets. Many people hate thinking and talking about this topic, but getting your estate planning done correctly adds a layer of protection and peace of mind for your family and your future. If you don't have a spouse or children yet, you can skip those last two recommendations for a will and term life insurance. However, keep them in the back of your mind in case the day ever comes, and you need the coverage.

Trusts (The Probate Shortcut)

A Revocable Living Trust is an alternative to a will, often created alongside a "Pour-Over" Will as a comprehensive estate plan. Trusts allow you to transfer assets (such as your home and brokerage accounts) to the trust while you are alive, bypassing the lengthy, public, and expensive probate process upon your death. Trusts also allow you to set specific conditions on how and when your heirs receive money (e.g., at age 25, or over the course of 10 years), and they ensure your finances are managed privately if you become incapacitated. Consult an estate planning attorney if your estate includes any real estate, a net worth over $500,000 in non-retirement assets, and/or complex family dynamics. Estate laws are highly state-specific. Probate limits, costs, and procedures vary significantly by state. While online templates can be useful for simple situations, a local estate attorney is the best defense against invalidating your documents due to state-level technicalities.

Case Study: A Tale of Two Estates

Scenario A (The Will - "The Hard Way")

Paul loses a parent who only had a Will. He spends 9–12 months in probate court, pays 3–5% of the estate value in legal fees, and cannot access the funds to pay the mortgage on the house, forcing him to pay out of pocket to keep the lights on.

Scenario B (The Trust - "The Smart Way")

Marge loses a parent who set up a Revocable Living Trust. She gains access to the accounts in 1–2 weeks, pays zero court fees, and privately transfers the home title without a judge, preserving the full inheritance.

Advanced Strategies

Shop Annually

Compare quotes on reliable sites such as PolicyGenius to save $100–$500/year on auto or home insurance. Many companies offer a significant discount when bundling your home and auto coverage.

Raise Deductibles

With a $1,000+ emergency fund in place, increase deductibles (e.g. , $1,000 to $2,500) to lower your premiums typically by 10–20%.

Umbrella Policies

For approximately $200 to $300 per year (though it can creep near $400 for people with risk factors such as swimming pools, multiple properties, or teen drivers), you can add a $1 million personal umbrella policy to your insurance portfolio. This coverage should be considered a non-negotiable once your net worth exceeds $500,000. An umbrella policy acts as a massive financial forcefield, protecting not just your current assets (like your home and index funds), but your future earnings from devastating lawsuits that easily exhaust standard auto and home limits. It is also essential for those who own rental properties or serve on nonprofit boards (though you should always check if the nonprofit carries Directors & Officers insurance for you first).

Important Note: To qualify for an umbrella policy, most insurers require you to first increase the liability limits on your auto and home insurance to their maximums (typically 250/500/100 for auto and $300,000 for home). It is highly recommended to purchase your umbrella policy from the same insurer that provides your auto and home insurance to avoid any coverage gaps.

Disability Insurance

If you are a W-2 employee, verify that your employer provides Long-Term Disability (LTD) insurance. If they do not, or if you are self-employed, consider purchasing a private policy that replaces at least 60% of your income (e.g., $1,500/year for $60,000 coverage) to cover unexpected illness or injury. Being able to work and earn an income is your greatest wealth building asset and should be protected.

Action Steps

- **Log in to your bank and retirement accounts today to verify your beneficiaries are officially listed.**
- **Consider requesting a quote to raise your auto insurance deductible to $1,000 to see how much you save.**

CHAPTER 7

Debt Management

Debt can feel like an inescapable trap, but it's a challenge you can overcome. With a clear plan, you can turn your debt around and, in time, use that money as a stepping stone to financial freedom.

This chapter helps you understand why debt management matters then introduces ways to eliminate high-interest debt, build solid credit habits, and highlight pitfalls to avoid.

Why Debt Management Matters

High-interest debt (above 6% APR, excluding your primary mortgage) grows faster than most investments, draining your wealth-building ability and weakening your financial stability. Consider your mortgage an essential housing expense that you can address later, even if the current rate is 6% or higher. It is not an urgent fire that must be put out immediately. Alternatively, a $5,000 credit card debt at 25% interest *costs* you an additional $1,250 a year in interest, while a $5,000 investment at 7% *earns* you $350. Paying off high-interest debt first frees up cash for things that matter most to you. Additionally, maintaining strong credit habits and managing specific debts, like student loans, can boost your overall credit score, potentially saving thousands on future loans, such as home equity lines.

Know Your Debt

List all debts: current balance, interest rate, minimum payment, and due date. Focus on high-interest debt (e.g., 25% credit cards) rather than low-interest debt (e.g., 5.25% car loans or 4.5% mortgage).

Payoff Strategies

The Debt Avalanche (The Math Method)

Attack the debt with the highest interest rate first, while paying only the minimums on the rest. Mathematically, this approach saves you the most money in total interest. It is ideal for highly analytical people who want to mathematically optimize their interest savings.

The Debt Snowball (The Momentum Method)

Ignore the interest rates and attack the smallest dollar balance first. When that debt is paid off, roll its payment into the next-smallest balance. This creates a psychological snowball effect. It is ideal for people who need quick, visible wins to stay motivated.

For example, if you have an **$800 medical bill, a $2,500 credit card bill, a $5,200 car loan,** and a **$20,000 student loan**, you would attack the medical bill first, regardless of the interest rate for each loan. Throw every extra dollar at that $800 balance while paying only the minimums on the others. Once the medical bill is gone, roll that entire payment into the credit card bill. Once the credit card balance is $0, move the extra money each month into your car loan until that balance reaches $0. And finally, move the combined total to the student loan until you are completely debt-free. If you were using the Avalanche method, you would ignore the $800 medical bill and attack the 25% credit card debt first, since that would save you the most money in interest.

Even though the credit card likely has a much higher interest rate, the

Snowball method prioritizes the psychological win of erasing that $800 balance. Both methods require temporarily sacrificing some guilt-free spending, but the relief of being debt-free and unburdened by bills makes it worthwhile in the end.

> **The Employer Match Rule:** Before you spend every extra dollar on your credit card debt, make sure you're contributing enough to your 401(k) to receive your employer's full match. Doing so essentially doubles your initial investment (once fully vested), and almost no consumer debt interest rate can beat that.

Grey Zone Debts

Debts with interest rates between 3.5% and 6% are in the 'Grey Zone.' Mathematically, you might be better off investing the extra cash, as historical market returns of 7–10% annually usually beat the cost of this debt. But personal finance is never just about numbers; it's also psychological. If being free and clear from debt gives you more peace of mind than potentially squeezing a few extra percentage points out of an index fund, paying it off is an excellent choice. In the Grey Zone, there are no wrong answers—only the answer that best fits your situation and personality.

Credit Basics: Building a Strong Foundation

Your credit score is like a financial report card; it helps determine how much you'll pay for various loans. For young adults just starting out, building good credit early can save thousands of dollars over a lifetime. Let's break down how credit is calculated, the best ways to build it, and traps to avoid so you can set yourself up for success.

How Credit Scores Are Calculated

Credit scores (typically 300–850, with FICO being the most common) reflect your borrowing and repayment habits. Here's what goes into your score:

Payment History (35%): Paying bills on time, even if only the minimum amount is paid, is the biggest factor. A single late payment can drop your score by 50–100 points.

Credit Utilization (30%): The percentage of your available credit that you're using. It's best to keep utilization below 30% (e.g., $300 on a $1,000 limit), ideally under 15% month-to-month.

Length of Credit History (15%): Longer accounts boost your score. Keep old accounts open, even if unused.

Types of Credit (10%): A mix of credit cards, loans, or mortgages helps, but don't overdo it.

New Credit Inquiries (10%): Applying for too many accounts in a short time can hurt your score, as it can signal financial instability to lenders.

A score above 740 is "very good," unlocking lower interest rates. Below 670? You'll pay more for loans, or you'll likely struggle to qualify. 800-850 is considered exceptional and typically gets the best rates.

Note: Credit scoring models (like FICO and VantageScore) are complex. The point drops and the increases mentioned here are estimates based on typical scenarios. Your actual score changes will depend on your unique credit profile.

Best Ways to Build Credit

Explore Secured Credit Cards: Apply with Visa, Mastercard, or Capital One to get a card with no yearly fee. Use it for small purchases (e.g., gas) and pay in full monthly. Use NerdWallet.com to compare various credit card options.

Pay Bills on Time: Set up auto-pay for utilities or rent (if reported to credit bureaus). On-time payments are your score's best friend.

Keep Utilization Low: Remember the rule from above. Keep your monthly charges well under that 30% threshold and pay them off before the statement closes.

Monitor Your Score: Use free tools like Credit Karma or Experian to track progress monthly.

Become an Authorized User: Ask a trusted friend or family member with good credit to add you as an Authorized User on their card. Their payment history boosts your score, but it is critical to ensure that they're responsible, as their future defaults will negatively impact your score.

Pitfalls to Avoid

Missing Payments: A 30-day late payment can tank your score and stay on your report for seven years. Set calendar alerts or auto-pay to stay on track.

Maxing Out Cards: High utilization signals risk to lenders. If you hit 80% utilization on a $1,000 limit, your score could drop by 50 points.

Closing Old Accounts: Shutting down your first card shortens your credit history, hurting your score. Keep it open with a small, recurring charge (e.g., Netflix or Spotify).

Applying for Too Many Cards: Each application triggers a "hard inquiry," dinging your score by 5–10 points. Limit applications to one every six months.

"Buy Now, Pay Later" (BNPL): Avoid these altogether. They often don't help build your credit score, but they can lead to overspending traps.

Ignoring Errors: Mistakes on your credit report (e.g., wrong balances) can lower your score. Check reports annually at AnnualCreditReport.com and dispute errors.

Example: Tara's Credit Climb

Tara, a 31-year-old office manager for a small local company earning $58,000, had no credit history, making it tough to qualify for apartments. She got a Discover secured card with a $1,500 deposit, used it to buy $350 in groceries each month, and paid it off immediately. She added Experian Boost to report her $900 rent payments. Within a year, her score hit 690, qualifying her for a $2,500 unsecured card and a lease without a co-signer. "Building credit felt like unlocking a cheat code," she said. Now, she's eyeing a car loan at a lower rate.

Know Your Loan

Not all loans work this way. For example, credit cards calculate interest daily and often have variable rates that can change without notice. Adjustable-rate mortgages (ARMs) can also change unpredictably. While student loans and traditional fixed-rate mortgages are typically amortized loans, understanding how interest accumulates for each loan early on is essential.

Every percentage point matters. Over time, it adds up in a big way, whether to your benefit or to the lender's. The earlier you learn to spot the difference and act, the less debt you will incur in the long run.

Why Loan Interest Hits Hard at the Start

If you've taken out an auto loan, mortgage, or student loan, chances are you've dealt with what's called an **amortized loan**. While your monthly payment remains the same throughout the loan, the make up of that payment changes significantly over time. The lender calculates your interest owed each month based on the remaining principal balance. Because the principal is the highest for payment one, the interest is also at its highest charged amount, with payments going mostly towards the interest owed and only a fraction to the actual principal. As time goes on, the principal amount slowly overtakes the interest amount owed.

Let's break it down with an example.

Example: $50,000 Loan at 7% Interest

- Imagine you take out $50,000 in student loans at a 7% interest rate on a 10-year term.
- Your monthly payment would be about $580.
- In your first payment, about $292 goes toward interest. That means nearly half your payment isn't even touching the debt itself.
- After 5 years of payments, you've paid around $35,000 total, but you've only reduced the balance by about $21,000. The rest? It went to interest.
- This underscores why it's crucial to hit these loans hard as early as possible.

Why You Need to Act Early

Every extra dollar you pay toward principal early in the loan reduces the total interest you pay over time. Even small additional payments towards the principal can save you thousands over time.

Except in cases where the costs of refinancing outweigh the benefits of the lower rate, it's always smart to refinance loans to a lower interest rate. A drop from a 7% to a 5% interest rate loan could save you over $4,000 in interest over the life of the loan. That is real money that stays in your pocket instead of disappearing into the bank's balance sheet.

Student Loans: Navigating a Major Debt Type

If you're one of the 45 million Americans carrying student loan debt, you're not alone, and there's a smart way to handle it. Whether you're just out of college or managing loans from years ago, understanding federal versus private loans and how to prioritize payments can transform this debt from a burden into a manageable part of your financial plan. Let's break it down so you can stay on track.

Federal vs. Private Loans

Student loans come in two options: federal (from the government) and private (from banks or lenders). Knowing the difference helps you strategize repayment:

Federal Loans

Pros: Fixed rates (e.g., 5–7%), flexible repayment plans (e.g., income-driven repayment capping payments at 10–20% of income), and forgiveness options (e.g., Public Service Loan Forgiveness after 120 qualifying payments for teachers, nurses, etc.)

Cons: Higher rates than some private loans for high-credit borrowers; complex forgiveness rules.

Types: Subsidized (no interest while in school) and unsubsidized (interest accrues immediately).

Private Loans

Pros: Potentially lower rates for strong credit (e.g., 4–6% fixed or 3–5% starting variable); faster payoff with aggressive payments.

Cons: Variable rates can spike; fewer protections (no income-driven repayment plans or forgiveness); stricter eligibility requirements.

Note: Avoid private loans that prohibit early payoff, as they lock you into paying full interest even if you can clear the balance sooner. Check loan terms for "prepayment penalties" before signing.

Refinancing Options: Refinancing replaces existing loans with a new one, ideally at a lower rate and better terms. A good rule of thumb is that new rates are at least 1% lower than your current rate. If you have a stable income and a credit score above 700, refinancing can drastically cut your monthly payments.

Accelerating Your Student Loan Payoff

Once you understand your loan type and have explored your refinancing options, you should look to pay off your student loans as efficiently as possible. Consider the following strategies:

- **Employer Educational Assistance:** Ask your company's HR department if they offer a qualified educational assistance program. These programs can provide up to $5,250 per year in income tax-free benefits toward student loan repayment.

- **Income-Driven Repayment (IDR) Plans:** Borrowers with federal student loans can explore IDR plans, which set monthly payments based on income and family size. These plans may offer lower payments and eventual forgiveness for the remaining balance after 20 to 25 years.

- **Absence of Prepayment Penalties:** Be aware that federal law prohibits lenders from charging penalties for paying off student loans early, regardless of whether they are federal or private. This means you can increase your payments at any time to pay down your principal faster.

- **Maximize Extra Payments:** Paying more than the minimum can substantially reduce the total interest you pay over the life of the loan. Instruct your servicer to apply these extra funds directly to the principal balance to maximize your savings and accelerate your payoff date.

Where to Look: Check lenders like SoFi, Earnest, or Credible for rates

(5-10 minutes online). Compare fixed vs. variable rates; fixed is safer in a rising-rate environment.

Risks: Refinancing federal loans into private loans forfeits eligibility for forgiveness or deferment. It is a permanent, irreversible decision. Weigh this change carefully before chasing down a slightly lower interest rate.

Tip: Shop with multiple lenders within 14 days; credit bureaus count it as a single inquiry to minimize score impact.

Case Study: Marcus's Turnaround

Marcus, 34, a journeyman electrician earning $79,000 a year, struggled with $20,000 in high-interest loans at 12% and $8,000 in credit card debt at 24%. Using the debt avalanche method, Marcus allocated $1,200 per month to the credit card debt, clearing it in 8 months and saving over $750 in interest. He negotiated with his loan provider, reducing the interest rate to 8%, which saved him almost $1,000 annually. In two years, he paid off half his loans and boosted his credit score to 740. "Planning turned debt into opportunity," he said. Marcus now uses Empower to track expenses monthly, ensuring every dollar supports his goals.

Leveraging Consolidation and Negotiation

You've learned to manage high-interest debt using the avalanche or snowball method; now, improve your repayment strategy with debt consolidation and creditor negotiation. Consolidation only works if you stop using the credit cards you just paid off. Many people consolidate, then max out the cards again, increasing their debt.

These intermediate strategies can help lower rates, simplify payments, and save hundreds, turning debt into a manageable stepping stone in today's high-cost world.

How to Consolidate and Negotiate

1. **Explore Consolidation:** Apply for a personal loan (e.g., SoFi, 7–10% rates) to replace higher-interest debts. Ensure the term is 3–5 years to avoid stretching payments.

2. **Call Creditors:** Politely ask for a rate reduction or fee waiver, citing on-time payments. A 2% rate drop on a $5,000 card saves $100/year.

3. **Compare Offers:** Use platforms like Credible to find the best loan rates. Avoid balance transfer cards with high fees (3–5%).

4. **Monitor Credit:** Check your score on Credit Karma or Experian to ensure consolidation boosts it.

Important Tax Note: If you successfully negotiate to settle a debt for less than what you owe, the IRS may consider the forgiven amount as taxable income. You could receive a Form 1099-C at tax time. Be sure to set aside funds to cover this potential tax bill.

Action Steps

- List all student loans (federal/private, rates, terms) tonight.
- Check for prepayment penalties on private loans this week.
- Research refinancing rates on Credible or SoFi if your credit score is 700+.
- Build a one-month emergency fund before extra loan payments.
- Explore income-driven plans at StudentAid.gov for federal loans.

CHAPTER 8

Investing Basics

Saving your way to financial freedom in regular checking or savings accounts is almost impossible. Thanks to the invisible thief of inflation, the $1,000 sitting idle in a standard checking account today might only buy about $970 worth of groceries next year. By keeping your money in a regular checking account you aren't 'staying even'—you are actively falling behind. Historically, investing has been the most reliable way to outpace inflation and build a solid foundation towards a comfortable retirement and financial freedom.

Time is your greatest asset. Because of compound interest, waiting just 10 years to start can mean you have to save *twice* as much every month to reach the same goal. Seeing the math when you choose to delay starting to invest is brutal. However, there is a massive opportunity: a recent study found that 40% of American adults have no retirement savings, and 50% are not actively saving for retirement at all. By starting today, you aren't just catching up; you are already ahead of nearly half the population!

Getting Started

Before you begin investing, you need to understand the two main retirement accounts available to you. Knowing how each one works will ensure your money works just as hard as you do!

The Core Difference

A 401(k) is an employer-sponsored plan that often includes a match on a certain percentage of your contributions (typically 50%-100%). The contributions for a 401(k) are done pre-tax out of your paycheck. A Roth IRA is an individual account you open yourself that allows for tax-free withdrawals in retirement since your contributions are made post-tax.

Grab "Free" Money

If your job offers a 401(k) match, contribute enough to get the full match. A 3% match on $50,000 is $1,500 in extra cash each year, effectively doubling the initial investment. In 2026, you can stack up to $24,500 in a 401(k). However, be aware of your company's vesting schedule. Many employers require you to stay with the company for a minimum number of years (often 2 to 5); if you leave early, you may forfeit the unvested portion of the match.

50+ Boost

- If you are age 50 or older, you can contribute an extra $8,000 (total: $32,500).

Open an Account

Use Vanguard, Fidelity, or another trusted investing site for low-cost brokerage or retirement accounts. A **Roth IRA** offers tax-free growth (up to $7,500 in 2026, or $8,600 if you are 50+), while a taxable brokerage gives flexibility.

Important Note for High Earners: If you are a single filer and your modified adjusted gross income (MAGI) is above $168,000 ($252,000 limit if married filing jointly; 2026 limits), you are legally prohibited from contributing directly to a Roth IRA. This amount reflects your total income after deductions like your 401(k) contributions. If you're close to these limits, consult a professional first. However, you can still achieve tax-free growth by using a Backdoor Roth IRA, which involves contributing to a Traditional IRA and then converting it promptly, or by maximizing a Roth 401(k) through your employer if available. More details are in Chapter 11.

Target Date Funds: Set It and Forget It

If the idea of trying to choose different stock buckets and manually rebalancing your portfolio regularly feels overwhelming, don't panic. There's a perfect, hands-off default way to invest for beginners.

Target Date Funds (TDFs) are mutual funds designed to simplify investing by automatically adjusting their asset allocation based on your planned retirement year. They are the ultimate "set it and forget it" tool for beginners and busy professionals alike.

How It Works: You choose a single fund aligned with the year you hope to retire (e.g., 2060 if you plan to retire around age 65). The fund is managed by professionals who instantly diversify your money across domestic stocks, international stocks, and bonds with varying aggressiveness depending on the target retirement year.

Even better, they automatically handle the "glide path" for you. The fund starts with a higher allocation to stocks for maximum growth when you are young, and automatically shifts toward bonds for stability as you get closer to retirement.

The Math in Action: Consider Jamie, a teacher earning $56,000 annually who hopes to retire around 2061. Instead of manually buying VOO,

VXUS, and BND separately, Jamie selects the Vanguard Target Retirement 2060 Fund (VTTSX).

Beginning at age 28, Jamie automates a $250 monthly transfer straight into this one fund. Right now, the fund automatically invests about 90% in stocks and 10% in bonds. By the time the year 2060 rolls around, it will have gradually shifted closer to 45% stocks and 55% bonds. Jamie gets all the benefits of a perfectly balanced, risk-managed portfolio without ever touching a spreadsheet or manually rebalancing a single thing.

Building Your Own Portfolio

While Target Date Funds are excellent, they often carry slightly higher fees. Some investors prefer to have full and total control over their money. If you are willing to do a little math and manually rebalance your accounts once a year, building your own low-cost portfolio is a proven, low-cost approach towards retirement—if structured correctly.

Choose Simple Investments

Investing doesn't require a finance degree or a fat wallet. **Research consistently shows that over 20 years, approximately 90% of professional fund managers fail to beat the S&P 500**. For the average person, the odds of beating the market are even lower, as high fees, emotional selling, and a lack of diversification in their portfolio cause the vast majority of people to significantly underperform a simple, low-cost index fund.

Select low-cost ETFs or index funds with expense ratios below 0.15 %. These are like baskets of various stocks that spread out your risk. To build a solid foundation, mix a few core categories: **Total Market** or **Large-Cap Blend** funds (your core foundation) for stability, and **Large-Cap Growth** funds for typically reliable momentum. From there, you can sprinkle in aggressive growth funds (**Small Caps**) for higher upside, **bonds** for income, and **international funds** to capture global growth outside the U.S.

You generally don't want these in equal parts; your most stable funds should carry the most weight. A solid baseline example for an investor with a long investment horizon (12+ years) could be 60% to Total Market or Large-Cap Blend, 30% to International, and 10% to Bonds.

If you have a higher tolerance for potential market volatility, you could add in large-cap growth and small-cap stocks to your portfolio breakdown. An example of how that would look would be 35% Total Market, 15% Large-Cap Growth, 15% Small-Cap, 25% International, and 10% Bonds. You can then review and adjust yearly. Do not sell off anything if you feel you have too much in a specific category. Simply adjust the purchase percentages for each category as needed.

For example, if you automate a $200 weekly investment, that translates to $120 to Total Market, $60 to International, and $20 to Bonds.
Or if you choose the more advanced route, $70 to your Total Market foundation, $30 to Large-Cap Growth, $30 to Small Caps, $50 to International funds, and $20 to Bonds. This plan ensures your core stays steady while still leaving room for solid upside returns. Examples of such funds include:

- **VOO** or **FSKAX**
  VOO (tracks the S&P 500, the largest U.S. companies, excellent diversification for your large-cap blend foundation). **FSKAX** (tracks the entire U.S. stock market).
  Note: To avoid heavy portfolio overlap, investors typically pick only one of these to act as their core foundation.

- **VUG** (large growth companies, great for a large cap growth bucket)

- **SCHD** (quality U.S. companies paying strong dividends, a great large-cap option)

- **VB** (tracks small-cap U.S. companies, bringing higher risk and higher upside for your aggressive growth bucket)

- **VXUS** (tracks total international stocks, giving you global exposure outside the U.S. to complete your international bucket)
- **BND** (tracks the total U.S. bond market, providing steady income and acting as a stabilizer when the stock market gets bumpy)

> **Quick Reminder:** The specific funds mentioned above (and elsewhere in the book) are just examples. They are not specific buy recommendations and were mentioned solely to show examples of broad-market diversified options for the mentioned bucket categories. Markets constantly change. Always do your own research or talk to a pro before investing your money.

The Pension Clause

If you have a pension (defined benefit plan) through a union or government job, absolutely count it toward your retirement goals, but don't rely on it 100%.

The Math: You can likely count your pension as 5% to 10% of your savings rate. This means you might only need to save 5% to 10% of your own paycheck into a Roth IRA to hit the total "15% Goal."

The Warning: Pensions die with you (typically), and they aren't liquid. A separate Roth IRA gives you money you can access for emergencies or pass down to your kids one day, giving you the best of both worlds: reliable additional funds and flexible cash.

Balanced Portfolio With Diversified Investing

Diversify Your Overall Portfolio

Now that you know exactly which stock and bond funds to look for, you have to decide how much of your total money goes into the "growth" engine (your stock buckets) versus the "stability" shock absorber (your bonds).

But how much of each? You need a **glide path**—an investment strategy that adjusts the percentages of your stock versus bond allocations as you get older and closer to retirement.

To find the right balance, I recommend taking a **"Two-Lane Highway"** approach based on your personal comfort with risk:

- **Lane 1: The Modern Wealth Builder (120 Minus Your Age).** Because people are living longer, this is the modern gold standard for investing. Subtract your age from 120 to find the percentage of your money that should be in stocks. This maximizes growth so your portfolio can outpace inflation during a 30-year retirement.

- **Lane 2: The Sleep-Well-At-Night Approach (110 Minus Your Age).** If market dips make you overly anxious, this is your lane. Subtracting your age from 110 gives you a slightly smaller stock percentage and a heavier bond allocation, reducing your day-to-day volatility.

The result of your chosen formula is the percentage of your money that should be in stocks for growth. The remaining portion goes into bonds, acting as a safety brake that automatically becomes stronger as you age.

The Math in Action: Let's say you are 30 years old and investing $500 a month.

- **Using the 120 Rule (Modern Wealth Builder):** 120 - 30 = 90. This means 90% of your money ($450) goes into your stock funds (VOO, VUG, VXUS, etc.), and 10% ($50) goes into your bond fund (BND).

- **Using the 110 Rule (Sleep-Well-At-Night):** 110 - 30 = 80. This means 80% of your money ($400) goes into your stock funds, and 20% ($100) goes into your bond fund (BND).

Then, you take that stock allocation ($450 or $400) and divide it across the four large-cap blend, large-cap growth, small-cap, and international buckets we discussed in the previous section.

The Power of Compound Interest Growth

If you're feeling defeated by how much to contribute to retirement, start with 3% and increase your contribution by 1% with every annual raise until you reach your 15% goal. In most cases, you won't even notice that 3% not hitting your bank account.

As noted above, compound interest is an incredibly powerful wealth-building tool. Let's consider the implications of investing 8% of a $50,000 salary, with a 3% employer match, in an S&P 500 index fund over 40 years.

Simple Breakdown

- **Your salary:** $50,000 per year.

- **You invest: 8%** = $4,000 per year.

- **Employer Match: 3%** = $1,500 per year.

- **Total yearly investment:** $4,000 + $1,500 = $5,500.

- **Time:** 40 years.

• **Assumed growth:** The S&P 500 typically grows about 7% per year after fees and inflation (a safe estimate).

What Happens?

If you invest $5,500 every year for 40 years and earn 7% compounded annually, your investment would grow to approximately $1,174,852. That's without even accounting for pay raises or increasing your investment percentage over the years! Even a modest 1% increase in your contributions would result in approximately $1,281,657 over 40 years. That's an extra $106,000+, greatly enhancing your financial future. Now imagine you average 2% or 3% yearly pay increases, contribute 10% or 12%, and receive the employer match.

Take control of your retirement by starting now; time and consistency are key to building wealth.

Understand Key Risks

- **Get Rich Quick Schemes**: As the old saying goes, "if something seems too good to be true, it probably is." Ignore the influencers and ads promising thousands of dollars or easy, guaranteed, quick returns. True wealth is built with patience over time. Most things that make someone rich instantly or in a short period of time are not investing; they're typically gambling.

- **Market Risk:** Stocks can drop due to economic shifts (e.g., the S&P 500 fell 18% in 2022 but rebounded by 2024). Until you are close to retirement age, stay the course and keep your money invested (subject to rebalancing). According to a J.P. Morgan report, returns for investors who missed the 10 best market days from 2010–2023 would have been 50% lower than those of other investors. (J.P. Morgan, 2023).

- **Concentration Risk**: Betting too much on one stock or sector (e.g., tech) can be detrimental if that sector crashes. Diversify with Index Funds and ETFs like VOO (S&P 500) or FSKAX (Total Market) for exposure to hundreds of companies across different sectors.

- **Panic Selling:** When the market drops, emotions run high, and too many people hit "sell." Instead, automate your investing with $200 per month (or whatever fits your budget) using dollar-cost averaging. Don't chase the highs or fear the lows. Check in quarterly or every 6 months, not when headlines scream. Long-term investing is about consistency, not emotion.

- **Liquidity Risk:** Some investments, like Certificates of Deposit (CDs) or certain private funds, lock up your money for months or years, meaning you face penalties or are strictly prohibited from withdrawing those amounts during that period. Keep your liquid emergency savings in a high-yield savings account (HYSA) instead.

- **Rebalance Yearly**: Do this every January to keep risk aligned with goals.

Action Steps

- Open a Vanguard or Fidelity account (30 minutes online).

- Check for a 401(k) employer match and contribute enough to get it.

- Verify your Phase 1 Starter Emergency Fund is fully funded, then automate $100+ per month to a low-cost ETF, such as VOO.

CHAPTER 9

Major Purchases & Life Events (Home, Car, Education)

Major, potentially life-altering purchases need to be dealt with greater consideration. A misstep here won't just stretch your budget—it can bury your financial future in decades of debt.

With housing and vehicle prices soaring, strategic planning helps ensure that these major expenses align with your goals rather than draining your finances. There are specific principles for such major items that need to be taken into consideration since even investing likely won't be able to bail you out. You need to make sure your "big-ticket" items fit within your income foundation with simple to follow percentage breakdown points.

To help protect yourself, implement **The 48-Hour Big Ticket Rule.** For everyday items over $100, try to wait 24 hours. But for major life purchases over $1,000, force yourself to wait at least 48 hours before making a final decision. This forced pause will help mute the emotional high of the moment, giving you the time to do objective research before committing a large amount of your hard-earned money and ultimately be left with buyer's remorse.

Why Strategic Planning Matters

Large purchases are exciting. Nobody is denying this. Whether it's planning to buy a new home, buying a car, the opportunity that comes with being accepted into an education program, or even planning a big wedding. However, without a plan, these things can end up trapping you in an endless paycheck-to-paycheck cycle.

Make purchases that support your future, not derail it, and be sure your decisions are tailored to your current needs. Every decision should be framed through a cost-benefit analysis.

For example, are the upfront costs and carrying (e.g., maintenance) costs avoided by renting more valuable to your situation than the equity you'd build through home ownership? Weigh each option thoroughly before diving in.

Big-Ticket Guardrails To Follow

Home Purchase

Most importantly, do not buy a home unless you plan to live there for at least 5 years. It takes roughly five years of living in the home for the property value to appreciate enough to simply break even on the fees it cost you to buy and sell it.

Once you are ready to buy, try to save 20% down to avoid private mortgage insurance (PMI), which adds hundreds to your monthly mortgage bill. If you are unable to put 20% down on your first home purchase, consider refinancing within a few years to eliminate PMI and lower monthly payments if interest rates drop.

Keep home payments (principal, interest, taxes, insurance) below 33% of net/take-home pay (e.g., $1,320 on $4,000 in net pay)**, preferably closer to 25%.** Use Zillow or Realtor.com to help track local prices and avoid overpaying for your next purchase.

The "Static Mortgage" Myth: The biggest misconception that first-time home buyers have is that their monthly housing costs will stay the same for the next 30 years. While your Principal and Interest may be locked in for the duration of your loan, your Escrow, which covers property taxes and homeowners' insurance, is unpredictable and often increases each year.

The Escrow Reality

When you receive your monthly bill, it is actually four separate costs bundled together (often called **PITI**):

1. **P**rincipal: Paying back the loan. (Fixed)
2. **I**nterest: The cost of borrowing. (Fixed)
3. **T**axes: City and county property taxes. (Variable)
4. **I**nsurance: Your homeowners' policy premium. (Variable)

Why Payments "Randomly" Increase

Lenders recalculate your escrow account annually. If your city or town increases property taxes or your insurance provider raises premiums, your monthly payment will climb to cover the difference.

1. **The Assessment Trap:** Cities and towns can "reassess" your home's value to a higher price point based on state-mandated reassessment schedules. Some states reassess yearly and some every 2-6 years. Most reassess after every home sale. As a result, your city property tax bill and your mortgage payment can jump by hundreds of dollars overnight.

2. **The Insurance Spiral:** Natural disasters, rising construction costs, and inflation cause insurance companies to hike premiums. Even if you never file a claim, your payment increases because the cost to rebuild your home has gone up in that given area.

The Escrow Shortage Penalty

If your taxes or insurance go up mid-year, your lender pays the bill for you, but it creates a "shortage" in your account. To fix this, the lender will usually give you two options, both of which are painful:

- **The Lump Sum:** Pay the thousands of dollars you are "short" immediately.
- **The Double-Hike:** They spread the shortage over the next 12 months. This means your new payment includes the **permanent increase** plus a **temporary surcharge** to pay back the debt.

Refinancing: The 1% Rule vs. The Reset Trap

The 1% Rule for Lower Rates: If you already own your home, refinancing your mortgage to a lower interest rate can save you tens of thousands over the loan's lifetime. A good guideline is to consider refinancing when you can reduce your current interest rate by at least 1%. Still, always calculate your break-even point (total closing costs divided by your monthly savings) and make sure you plan to stay in the house long enough to recover those upfront costs.

The "Reset" Warning: Do not fall into the trap of constantly refinancing to chase a lower monthly payment. Every time you refinance into a new 20- or 30-year loan, you reset your amortization schedule. This pushes you right back to paying mostly interest instead of principal. If you refinance too many times, you will be trapped in a perpetual mortgage loop and never actually own your home. If you choose to refinance halfway through your mortgage, opt for a 10 or 15-year term so you don't lose the time you've already put in.

Automobile Purchase

Buying a flashy, brand-new car is one of the most common financial mistakes that keeps many people broke.
A $50,000 car loan at 6% over five years costs roughly $7,900 in interest, while new cars typically depreciate 20-30% in their first year, with the steepest drop in the first few months. Buying certified pre-owned vehicles that undergo rigorous inspections and driving them for several years maximizes value retention, minimizes depreciation costs, and ensures reliability at lower upfront costs. To protect your wealth, try your best to adhere to these rules:

- **The Used-Car Discount**: Look into buying certified pre-owned. Let someone else take the brutal 20% to 30% depreciation hit the moment the car drives off the lot.

- **The 15% Cap**: Your total monthly transportation costs (loan payment + insurance + gas + maintenance) must stay strictly below 15% of your net monthly income, **preferably closer to 10%.**

- **Minimum 20% Down Payment:** Put a minimum of 20% of the automobile's price down. The more you are able to comfortably put towards the down payment, the better.

- **The 60-Month Max Rule**: Avoid stretching an auto loan past 60 months. If you need a 72- or 84-month loan to afford the monthly payment, you cannot afford the car. Period. Aim for 36 to 48 months (or less) whenever possible, with 60 months as your max loan length.

- **Drive It For 6-10 Years:** When you purchase a reliable vehicle, plan to drive it for 6 to 10 years before considering a replacement.

Doing so will direct years' worth of car payments into investments or high-yield accounts.

The 48% Rule: The Sliding Scale Tradeoff

While your ***maximum*** amounts are 33% for housing and 15% for transportation, real-life situations call for flexibility, especially in expensive cities. If you need to break one rule, you should adjust the other proportionally. Your combined housing and transportation costs should stay within a strict limit and **never exceed 48% of your net income.**

The budget is like a seesaw; if one side goes up, the other must go down to keep it balanced. If you live in a high-cost-of-living area (like NYC or Los Angeles) and spend 40% of your income on rent, you can't just ignore the math. You have two realistic options to stay on track:

- **Option 1: The Commuter Trade-Off.** Move farther from the city, weighing your commute time against your overall rent savings to stay under the 33% housing threshold.
- **Option 2: The Sliding Scale.** If you choose an expensive apartment that takes up 40% of your net income, you must limit your transportation costs to 8% or less to stay within your budget. While you can afford the high rent, this means you'll need to take public transportation, ride a bike, or drive a paid-off, affordable car to remain financially secure.

Exceeding the 33% and 15% Limits

If your fixed costs for home and auto go over these limits, you are likely "house poor" or "car poor," meaning you spend so much on housing or car expenses that you have little cash left for other essential needs. In that case, you don't have an investing problem; you have a cash-flow problem. If this is the case, don't worry about the "Payoff vs. Invest" math yet. Instead, focus on stabilizing your budget, increasing your income, or downsizing these assets to return to the safe zone. Once your foundation is solid, you can aggressively pay down your loans or build your investment portfolio. Remember, 48% combined is an absolute max. 35% combined is the actual target.

Education: Buying the Right Degree

If you have kids approaching college years, or if you plan to attend grad school soon, remember that a college degree is another financial tool, and every tool has a price at which it no longer makes sense to buy. In a world where a four-year in-state public college degree can cost $140,000 but the average starting salary sits at $60,000, you must bridge that gap with a practical strategy, not just hoping for the best and dealing with the issue later.

- **The 1x Rule:** A sustainable rule of thumb is to keep total student loan debt at a 1-to-1 ratio of your expected first-year salary. The farther you cross that threshold, the more you are over-leveraging your future instead of investing in it. Being below 1x of your expected first-year salary is ideal.

- **The Community College Hack:** Consider attending a community college for the first two years to complete all gen-ed and core courses, then finishing at a college or university for a specific degree. Alternatively, target high-growth fields to ensure your debt-to-income ratio doesn't leave you 'degree-rich' but 'cash-flow dead' for the next twenty years.

The Elaborate Wedding Trap

Before saying 'I do', many couples unintentionally bury their financial future under a mountain of unnecessary floral arrangements and catering costs. The average U.S. wedding now costs over $32,000, and many couples use debt, often high-interest debt like credit cards, to cover the cost.

You are celebrating the start of a new life together, not the end of some treasure hunt. Don't sabotage your first major shared financial goal **for one expensive day**. Make the celebration memorable while keeping your future secure. Prioritizing a lavish event over a strong financial start is poor risk management. Your marriage is an investment; treat it that way by keeping the wedding budget reasonable and starting your life together without major debt.

Profile: The Regional Hub Couple

- **Ages:** 28 and 30
- **Combined Net Income:** $105,000 ($8,750 per month)
- **Location:** 90 minutes outside a major metro area

Implementing The 33% Housing Guardrail (Target 28% : Max 33%)

Target Monthly Payment: $2,450

- **The Math:** At a 6.3% interest rate, a $2,450 monthly budget supports a roughly **$400,000 home** (assuming 20% down and $500 per month set aside for property taxes and insurance).
- **The Reality:** While their absolute maximum ceiling is 33% ($2,888), targeting 28% prevents them from becoming house poor. In regional hubs, $400,000 still secures a solid starter home or townhouse. Within a metro core, this same payment often barely covers a 2-bedroom rental.

Implementing The 15% Transportation Guardrail (Target: 12% | Max: 15%)

Target Monthly Total: $1,050

- **The Breakdown:**
  - **Insurance:** $250 ($125/vehicle average)
  - **Maintenance:** $100 ($50 per month per vehicle)
  - **Fuel/Electric:** $200
  - **Remaining for Loan Payments:** $500
- **The Reality:** While the absolute ceiling is 15%, keeping it at 12% provides excellent balance. This $1,050 budget easily accommodates one solid car payment of $500, provided the second vehicle is older and paid in full.

Implementing A 12% Retirement Target

Monthly Investment: $1,050

- **The Strategy:** Following Step 8, this allocation meets the minimum wealth-building velocity.
- **Long-Term Impact:** Investing $1,050 monthly at a 7% annual return would result in approximately **$1.28 million** after 30 years.

Action Steps

- **Calculate your absolute maximum housing budget using the 33% rule.**

- **Look up the Kelley Blue Book value of your current vehicle.**
- **Check with your HR department if they offer a qualified educational assistance program.**

CHAPTER 10

Taxes and Keeping More of Your Money

Have you ever looked at your paystub and wondered where a third of your money went? With a few strategic, perfectly legal moves, you can better shield your money and keep more of your hard-earned cash. In this chapter, we'll break it down in simple terms, showing you some basic ways to lower your taxes and put that money toward your goals. Whether you're just starting or ready for a bit more help, these habits turn taxes from a headache into a tool for building wealth.

Why Tax Planning Matters

Taxes aren't just random numbers on a form; they're part of your everyday money flow. Every dollar you can save on taxes means more for yourself. For example, putting $6,000 into a 401(k) if you're in a common tax bracket (like 24%) could save you about $1,440 right away. Over 20 years at 7% annual growth, just that single year's $1,440 tax savings grows to about $5,500—that's tax-deferred growth on money you legally shield from the IRS. The key? Start small and focus on what you can control.

Core Tax-Saving Strategies

To keep things straightforward, we'll focus on easy wins that almost anyone can try, without getting lost in fancy terms.

401(k)

This is a retirement account offered by your employer. You put money in before taxes, so it lowers your current tax bill. For 2026, you can add up to $24,500 (or more if you're over 50). Note that IRS limits typically adjust annually for inflation. If you earn $70,000 and put in $8,000, you're only taxed on $62,000 income. That could save you $1,760 if you're in the 22% bracket. Check with your boss or HR department if they match some of what you put in—ALWAYS try to maximize your match (refer to Chapter 8 for the math).

Health Savings Account (HSA)

Think of an HSA as the ultimate, government-approved wealth-building tool. Known as 'The Unicorn' account, it boasts a Triple-Tax Superpower: your money goes in tax-free, it grows tax-free, and you withdraw it tax-free for medical expenses. It is the only account in the U.S. tax code that offers this triple threat. In 2026, an estimated 85% of employers offer contributions to Health Savings Accounts (HSAs), according to HSA Bank's Health & Wealth Index.

The Catch: To legally open an HSA, you must be enrolled in a **High-Deductible Health Plan (HDHP)**. These insurance plans typically have lower monthly premiums, but require you to pay more out-of-pocket before the insurance kicks in. In 2026, you can add up to $4,400 if single (or $8,750 for families). It's a smart way to prepare for doctor visits while cutting your tax bill. HSA funds never expire. Even if you change jobs or careers, the money can stay in the account and continue to grow.

Record Keeping: Always save your medical receipts and "Explanation of Benefits" (EOB) statements in a digital folder. During an audit, the IRS requires proof that HSA withdrawals were used for qualified expenses.

HSA Case Study: The $190k Couple

Meet Julie (37) and Mike (38). They earn a combined **$190,000** and are in the 22% federal tax bracket.

The Strategy: They choose the high-deductible health plan at Mike's job because they are relatively healthy. They decide to **max out** the family contribution of **$8,750** for 2026.

1. **The Employer "Seed":** Mike's company contributes $1,000 to his HSA as an incentive, meaning Mike and Julie save that $1,000 and only have to invest $7,750 of their own funds to reach the max.

2. **Instant Tax Savings:** By directly contributing $7,750 into their HSA, they immediately lower their taxable income to $182,250. This saves them roughly $1,925 in federal taxes alone.

3. **The Investment:** Instead of spending that $8,750 on aspirin or other medical-qualifying products, they pay for their $400 of annual medical costs out of pocket, while taking a picture of any bills and uploading them to their medical bill computer folder. They invest the full $8,750 in a **Total Stock Market Fund (FSKAX)**.

4. **The Result:** If they do this every year for 20 years at just a 7% return, they are estimated to have over **$358,000** in tax-free income for healthcare in retirement. If they reach age 65 and don't need it for health, they can withdraw it for *anything* (though they'd pay regular income tax then, just like a 401(k)).

Maximize Your Roth IRA

A **Roth IRA** eliminates future taxes. You contribute money from your paycheck that has already been taxed, it grows completely tax-free, and then you're ready to withdraw in retirement, which is also tax-free. A common strategy is to open a Vanguard (or another trusted investing site) Roth IRA and pick popular low-cost, broad market funds like VTI (with a tiny 0.03% fee). For 2026, the limit is $7,500 if your income qualifies (under $153,000 for single filers. Up to $168k for single filers for partial contribution). Automate up to $625 per month after you build your one-month emergency fund for essentials.

Charitable Donations

Because the IRS's Standard Deduction is currently so high, small charitable gifts won't actually lower the tax bill for most average earners—but that doesn't mean you shouldn't give! However, if you are a high earner or have significant property taxes and medical costs, itemizing your deductions allows you to deduct cash, clothing, or even old stock donations directly from your taxable income, making the donated dollar go further.

For example, a person in the 24% income tax bracket who makes a $1,000 charitable gift reduces their income tax bill by $240. The charity receives $1,000, but the donor effectively pays only $760. Use sites like Charity Navigator to pick good ones; it's both rewarding and practical.

1099 Contractors or Gig Workers

For 1099 contractors and gig workers (Uber, Etsy, Freelance), the IRS doesn't take taxes out of your check automatically. A common rule of thumb is moving 25%-30% of every payment into a separate 'Tax' HYSA immediately. Paying your estimated quarterly taxes ensures you aren't hit with a massive bill and underpayment penalties in April.

Action Steps

- **Check with HR to see if your health insurance is an HSA-eligible HDHP.**
- **Open a dedicated 'Tax Account' HYSA today if you are a 1099 gig worker.**

CHAPTER 11

Income Generation

Boost Your Salary: Unlock More Income

Time to start thinking of ways to boost your income. Earning more isn't just about working harder; it's about utilizing your skill set, earning certifications, and making strategic career moves when necessary. Investing in your own career can add thousands to your paycheck each week, giving you more to invest and ultimately enjoy.

Why Boosting Your Salary Matters

Increasing your income creates breathing room for your budget and fuels your savings. As previously mentioned, if you earn a $5,000 raise after taxes and invest just half of that raise yearly ($2,500/year) at a 7% annual return, you'll have over $34,000 extra in your pocket after 10 years. By upskilling, you're not just earning; you're building a wealth engine.

A recent LinkedIn study found that employees with in-demand skills (e.g., project management, data analysis) typically earned 10–20% more. Higher earnings compound your ability to hit big goals like a home down payment or early retirement without feeling the "pinch" in your daily life.

How to Boost Your Salary

To significantly boost your earning power, you may have to ignore the typical advice to 'follow your passion.' Instead, adopt the idea from Cal Newport's book *So Good They Can't Ignore You*: "passion is a byproduct of mastery, not a requirement for it." By consistently developing valuable skills—what Cal calls 'career capital'—you gain the power to set your own terms and salary. Don't just do what you love; become truly excellent at it, and the money will inevitably come.

- **Earn Certifications:** Invest in credentials that align with your field. A $500 course (e.g., PMP for project managers) can lead to a potential $7,000-$10,000 raise. Platforms like Coursera and Udemy offer affordable courses at $50–$200 in computer science, finance, coding, marketing, and leadership (among others). Sometimes your current company may cover the cost of advancement certifications. Check with your manager or HR for more information.

- **Take on More at Work:** Volunteer for high-visibility projects or roles. Leading a team or streamlining a process can position you for promotions. Ask your boss, "What can I take on to grow in this position?" A 5% raise on a $50,000 salary creates $2,500 annually for yourself that can be invested toward your future financial goals.

- **Learn New Skills:** Master in-demand skills based on your career field. Free resources like YouTube or low-cost platforms like Skillshare (starting at $10 per month as of 2026) make learning accessible. A new skill can often boost your value by 10% or more. Try searching "(fill in any topic) Masterclass" on YouTube to learn any topic you want from experts in that field.

- **Master Salary Negotiation:** Research your true market value on Glassdoor or Payscale. Practice asking for 10% above their initial offer. Use a firm, data-backed script: 'Based on my recent certifications and increased workload, the value I bring to XYZ Project, and using current market data for this role, I am seeking $X amount moving forward.' A single five-minute conversation backed up by facts can result in a $3,000 pay bump that pays you more per hour than years of side-hustling would have otherwise done. Similarly, Harvard research (2024) shows that simply initiating a negotiation boosts offers by an average of 7%.

- **Track Progress:** Log new skills or responsibilities monthly in a journal. When review time comes, present a clear case: "I led the XYZ project, saving 10 hours of manpower weekly." This can easily help justify a 5–10% raise.

Case Study: Cory's Career Leap

Cory, 35, an implementation manager earning $82,000, felt stuck in a mid-level role. He spent $300 on a Project Management Professional (PMP) certification through Coursera, studying for 10 hours per week for 3 months. He volunteered to lead a software rollout at work, saving his team 15 hours monthly. At his annual review, Cory used Glassdoor data to negotiate a $10,000 raise, citing his new skills and impact. To help avoid lifestyle creep, he automated 50% of after-tax earnings to a Vanguard Roth IRA, about $300 per month. "Upskilling opened doors I didn't know were even there," Cory said.

Consider an Active Side Hustle

Forbes reported that 39% of Americans have a side hustle, averaging $810 per month. That's $9,720 a year in your pocket. You could drive for Uber, sell crafts on Etsy, or freelance on Upwork. The key is to automate where that money goes—preferably to savings or investments—so it doesn't slip into daily wasteful spending.

For example, Maria, a 32-year-old nurse, started tutoring online for 10 hours a week, earning $300 per month which she funneled directly into her Roth IRA. But to truly scale her earnings, Maria can't just work more hours, otherwise she will eventually burn out. She needs to transition from active to passive income. By creating a digital nursing study guide to sell on Etsy, she can earn more money while she sleeps.

How to Scale and Build Passive Income

- **Add Passive Income:** Consider investing a few thousand into a dividend fund that has a solid history and that other trusted investors choose, like SCHD (3% yield) for $150/year or Publicly Traded REITs (which historically generate higher dividend yields for passive income). Reinvest any earnings.

- **Treat It Like a Business, Not a Hobby**: Keep your business and personal spending strictly separate from day one. Open a dedicated business checking account. While many freelancers eventually form an LLC for liability protection, you can often deduct legitimate business expenses as a Sole Proprietor right out of the gate. For example, $2,000 in software and home-office deductions saves you $480 in the 24% tax bracket. Consult a tax pro to see which structure is right for you.

- **Diversify:** Combine hustles (e.g., tutoring) with passive options (e.g., dividend funds) to help reduce risk.

Case Study: Diego's Income Surge

Diego, 25, a retail supervisor earning $45,000, made $200 per month selling fitness plans on Etsy. He scaled to $600 per month with video tutorials, earning $7,200/year. He invested $5,000 in Publicly Traded REITs, generating $400 in passive income per year. By treating his fitness side hustle as a true business, Diego was able to track and deduct roughly $2,500 in work-related software and home-office space expenses from his taxes. Since Diego is in the 12% tax bracket, doing this deduction saved him $300 at tax time.

Continuous Learning for Financial Wins

Knowledge is power, especially in finance. Stay sharp by following free resources like Reddit's r/personalfinance, podcasts like ChooseFI, or various YouTube channels like The Money Guys Show, Marko from Whiteboard Finance, and Ramit Sethi's I Will Teach You To Be Rich. These communities break down complex topics into bite-sized advice for working-class folks. I can attest that podcasts, YouTube series, books, and Reddit communities have personally provided enormous financial understanding and growth for myself.

Try to set aside 30-60 minutes a week to read or listen to a specific finance topic you're interested in. Small insights, like cutting one streaming service or negotiating your car insurance, can save hundreds annually.

Action Step

- **Research the cost of one professional certification in your field.**

CHAPTER 12

Allocate Windfalls Wisely

A windfall—an unexpected influx of cash such as a large bonus, inheritance, or a big tax refund—can feel like a golden ticket. But without a firm plan, that money can quickly disappear. The temptation to splurge on unnecessary purchases surges once those funds hit your bank account. Almost 50% of younger shoppers spend $100 or more in a single impulse buy triggered directly by social media feeds. This chapter explains how to allocate windfalls wisely to grow wealth and help prevent lifestyle creep. Instead of asking how to spend this found money, consider how you can use it to reach your financial independence goal even faster. We'll use a 75/25 split with clear steps to ensure every dollar works hard.

The 75/25 Windfall Split

- **75% Goals:** Pay off high-interest debt (e.g., 27% APR credit card), boost your emergency fund (ensure at least the amount of one month of essentials while aiming for 3-6 months' worth), or invest (e.g., VTI ETF in a Roth IRA).

- **25% Fun:** Spend on something enjoyable. This prevents burnout and keeps you motivated.

Example: For a $4,000 net bonus, allocate $3,000 to goals (e.g., $2,000 to debt, $1,000 to HYSA), $1,000 to fun (e.g., a weekend getaway).

Micro-Windfalls: The 60/40 Split

For smaller windfalls like a $200 birthday gift, $500 tax refund, or $125 side hustle payout, use a 60/40 split: 60% ($120) to your emergency fund or high-interest debt and 40% ($80) towards something fun for yourself. Set up an instant transfer to your HYSA via your bank's app (e.g., Ally's 30-second transfer) to lock in the 60% before spending. This builds momentum without feeling restrictive, even on tight budgets.

Avoiding Lifestyle Creep

A large one-time bonus shouldn't be wasted on a down payment for a luxury car that will likely cost you over $600 monthly payments for the next five years. Pre-commit your windfall to your goals before you spend it on a new recurring liability. Review Chapter 3 for budgeting tips.

Case Study: Elena's Windfall Strategy

Elena, a 40-year-old warehouse director earning $70,000 annually, received a $5,000 work bonus after a record-breaking quarter. Since bonuses are heavily taxed before being paid out, she ended up with $3,500. Determined to use this windfall wisely, she adopted the 75/25 allocation strategy. She directed 75% ($2,625) to her financial goals, splitting it between her Roth IRA contribution ($1,725) and bolstering her emergency fund in an Ally HYSA ($900). For the 25% ($875) allocated to lifestyle enhancements, Elena upgraded her phone and enjoyed a guilt-free night out with friends. By using the 75/25 framework, Elena balanced wealth-building and personal enjoyment, turning a one-time bonus into a foundation for long-term financial progress.

Action Steps

- **Write down your exact 75/25 game plan for your next expected tax refund.**
- **Set up a 'Fun Money' sinking fund so your 25% has a place to land.**

CHAPTER 13

Merging the Money: Strategies for Couples and Families

Money can help bring a family together or pull it apart. Whether you're a new couple combining finances for the first time or parents balancing kids' activity fees while protecting your own 'me money,' this section is for you. Recent data shows that money is the #1 stressor for most couples; a smart plan can turn your dollars into teamwork.

Why Family Finances Matter

Shared goals, like a dream home or paying for kids' college, help build trust, but clashing habits (one person saves, one spends) can cause tension. A recent Bankrate survey found 43% of couples argue about overspending, while over 60% of Americans live paycheck to paycheck. A system that combines budgets while allowing personal freedom for each partner keeps everyone happy, whether you're saving for a memorable family vacation or funding date nights. It's about being united on the things that matter.

How to Manage Family Finances

- **Hold a Monthly "Money Date":** Grab a coffee and spend 30 minutes reviewing finances with Honeydue. Set one shared goal (e.g., $10,000 for a trip) and one personal goal each (e.g., $200 for a golf lesson). It's less about spreadsheets and more about shared goals.

- **Merge Budgets with a Joint Account:** Open a joint checking account for shared expenses (rent, groceries, utilities) using the 60/20/20 framework from Chapter 3. Contribute proportionally based on your paychecks, say, 60/40 for a $60,000/$40,000 income split. Partner A would transfer enough to cover 60% of joint bills, while Partner B would transfer enough to cover 40% of the joint bills. Automate the paycheck transfers to make things easy and seamless. Test for 60-90 days to find the right fit for your situation.

- **Carve Out "Fun Money" for Autonomy**: Give each partner 5–10% of the net income for guilt-free spending. On a $4,000 monthly household income, that's $200–$400 each for hobbies or self-gifts with no judgment.

- **Align on Big Goals:** List three shared priorities (e.g., emergency fund, 529 plan, home fund, retirement). Use a sinking fund (Chapter 4) to save for those expected but irregular expenses. For a $5,000 vacation in two years, automate roughly $200 per month to a competitive HYSA. Check your progress during money dates to stay on track.

Financial Planning for Your Kids

The 529 Plan for Children

If you have children, set up a 529 plan for their future educational needs and plan to contribute to it regularly. A 529 plan is a tax-advantaged savings account designed to help pay for education expenses, such as college tuition or K–12 costs. Earnings grow tax-free, and withdrawals are also tax-free when used for qualified education expenses. If your child doesn't use the funds, up to $35,000 can be rolled over into their Roth IRA later, subject to IRS rules (e.g., must be open for at least 15 years, and the child must have earned income that year). With the Roth IRA contribution limit currently being $7,500, it will take several years to max out the $35,000 roll-over limit. This provides added flexibility so the funds can still benefit the child's future even if they choose to skip college.

The Childcare Reality Check

For many young families, the joy of welcoming a new child is often overshadowed by the shock of daycare costs. In many regions, monthly childcare expenses can match or even surpass your mortgage payment. If you aren't prepared, this significant new expense can completely disrupt your cash flow and force you to depend on credit cards to keep going.

- **How it fits your budget:** Childcare is a non-negotiable expense for working parents, meaning it clearly belongs in the 60% Essentials category of your 60/20/20 budget. If adding daycare causes your essential expenses to exceed 60%, you and your partner need to temporarily review and cut back on your 'Wants' to cover the difference. Remember, daycare is a temporary financial season; once your kids reach public school age, that cash flow will open back up.

- **The Dependent Care FSA Tip:** Many families unnecessarily pay for daycare using after-tax dollars when tax-advantaged options may be available to them. Check with your HR department to see if they offer a Dependent Care Flexible Spending Account (FSA). This account lets you set aside up to $5,000 of your income before taxes to cover eligible childcare, preschool, or summer day camps. By protecting that $5,000 from federal income taxes, a family in the 22% tax bracket saves an immediate $1,100 annually, money that stays in your bank instead of going to the IRS.

Teach Kids About Money

Involve kids in age-appropriate ways. For ages 5–12, one option is to use two mason jars: one for "fun money" to spend on things they want, and the other for savings to demonstrate how money grows as they earn from weekly chores. Each month, give them an extra $1 for every $10 saved to introduce the concept of interest. Once their savings jar reaches $50, transfer the funds to a custodial High-Yield Savings Account (HYSA) in their name. This provides them with a head start on a real account they can manage as they become teenagers. For teens, share a simplified budget to explain the trade-offs of skipping short-term luxuries for a long-term goal (e.g., "Skipping $100 of weekly takeout helps fund our family trip"). You can also consider introducing them to investing basics or their own youth checking account, both through custodial accounts.

Case Study: Sam and Taylor's Financial Harmony

Sam (31, teacher, $56,000) and Taylor (34, nurse, $79,000) used to clash over money. Sam squirreled away every dollar for a home, while Taylor's $500-per-month dining habit ate up their monthly budget. Using this system, they opened a joint checking account to cover their household 'Needs' (like rent and groceries). Because Taylor earns more, they fund this joint account using a 60/40 split, automatically transferring the funds every payday. Each kept $250 per month for fun. Monthly money dates with Honeydue aligned them on a $15,000 down payment for a home. By automating $500 per month to a SoFi HYSA, their balance grew to over $12,000 in two years. They started a $30-per-week 529 plan for their 6-year-old daughter, who now saves $5 a week of her own money in mason jars. "We're a team now, not rivals," Sam said, laughing about their old "budget battles."

Action Steps

- **Schedule a 30-minute 'Money Date' with your partner for this Sunday.**
- **Determine your household's exact percentage split for the 'Fun Money' category.**
- **Set up a 529 account if you have a child.**

Chapter 14

Mortgage Early Payoff vs Investing

Why Pay Off Your Mortgage Early?

Eliminating a mortgage offers significant flexibility by removing your biggest monthly expense. This freed-up cash flow can be redirected wherever you need it most while typically speeding up your wealth-building process. Without a mandatory housing payment, you have the freedom to change careers or adjust your lifestyle without the burden of a high monthly overhead.

Owning your home outright also offers invaluable peace of mind and security. It removes the risk of foreclosure, as long as you continue to pay property taxes and HOA dues, and provides a stable foundation unaffected by economic volatility or shifts in the job market. This psychological benefit creates a permanent safety net, ensuring your primary residence is a fully realized asset rather than a liability held by a lender.

To decide if this path is right for you, **apply the F2 Rule. Weigh the *Financials* of your interest rate against the *Feelings* of debt-induced stress.** From a mathematical standpoint, early payoff can generate substantial cost savings by minimizing interest paid on the loan. Because of how amortization works, even modest extra principal payments can save you tens of thousands of dollars over the life of the loan. Effectively, every dollar used to pay down the mortgage principal earns a guaranteed return equal to your interest rate, keeping more of your lifetime earnings in your own accounts.

How to Pay Off Your Mortgage Early

- **Extra Payments:** Add a fixed amount to each monthly payment (e.g., $100+) or make one extra payment annually to reduce principal faster.

- **Refinance Strategically:** If rates drop, especially if you can drop your rate by a full percentage point or more of your current rate, consider refinancing your mortgage to pay off faster without increasing monthly payments significantly.

- **Allocate Windfalls:** Once your emergency fund is firmly established, use bonuses, tax refunds, or side hustle income to make lump-sum payments toward the principal. Remember to set aside percentages for HYSA and investing as well.

- **Check Terms:** Confirm your lender allows early payoffs without penalties. Most modern mortgages do, but verify to avoid fees.

Investing Extra Funds: A Smarter Path to Mortgage Payoff for Low Rates

- **Capitalize on Low Rates**: If your mortgage rate is lower than 6%, historical market returns (around 7-10% annually for the S&P 500 or total market index funds) often outpace your interest rate, allowing your money to grow faster than the debt accrues. **NOTE:** Market returns are volatile and non-linear, whereas mortgage interest savings are guaranteed.

- **Liquidity and Safety**: Keeping extra funds in a brokerage account invested in low-cost index funds or ETFs provides easy access for emergencies, unlike locking it into your home equity, while still building toward a lump-sum payoff.

- **Wealth Building**: Over 10-20 years, compounded growth can cover your remaining mortgage balance and leave you with excess cash for other goals like retirement, charitable giving, or enjoying life debt-free.

How to Invest Towards Mortgage Freedom

- **Choose the Right Account:** Use a taxable brokerage account and consider investing the bulk in a total stock market index fund (e.g., VTI) or S&P 500 index fund (e.g., VOO) for broad diversification and low fees.
- **Contribute Consistently:** Redirect what you'd typically pay extra on your mortgage (e.g., $250 monthly) into your investments, automating transfers to capture dollar-cost averaging and ride out market volatility.
- **Monitor and Adjust:** Review annually; if markets underperform or rates rise, pivot back to extra payments. After 10-20 years, you can likely sell enough to pay off the remaining mortgage and keep the surplus.
- **Tax Considerations**: Gains may be taxed, but long-term capital gains rates are favorable. Consult a tax advisor to optimize your approach.

Why This Approach Matters

For mortgages at low rates, aggressively paying down principal ties up cash that could be invested elsewhere to earn more while remaining liquid if an emergency arises. This strategy maintains your path to debt freedom while preserving flexibility. Your money works harder, potentially accelerating other priorities..

Case Study: Alex and Jordan's Invest-to-Payoff Strategy

Alex (41, software engineer, $110,000) and Jordan (37, marketing specialist, $70,000) held a $300,000, 30-year mortgage at 4% interest beginning in 2024, with a monthly principal and interest payment of approximately $1,432.

Instead of adding extra funds to their mortgage principal, they decided to invest $250 monthly into an S&P 500 index fund starting in 2024, assuming an average 10% annual return (historical norm before factoring inflation, though not guaranteed).

After 20 years (in 2044):

- **Their Investment Grew to Approximately $182,000.**
- **Their Remaining Mortgage Balance: Approximately $141,000.**

At this 20-year milestone, Alex and Jordan had a choice. Because their investment account exceeded their debt, they used a large portion of the funds to make a lump-sum payment of the remaining $141,000. To cover the remaining balance and the capital gains taxes owed, they withdrew about $157,000 (paying approximately $16,000 in taxes) to pay off the mortgage in full. This left them with a $25,000 surplus in their brokerage account to jump-start their retirement and take a family vacation to celebrate their total debt freedom.

For comparison: If they had put that same $250 extra toward their mortgage principal each month starting in 2024, they would have paid off the house in about 22.5 years.

By choosing to invest instead, they reached "zero" debt 2.5 years faster (at Year 20 instead of Year 22.5). Also, applying that money directly toward the principal would have locked all their cash inside the house for two decades. By investing, they maintained total liquidity for 20 years, paid off the house faster, and generated an additional $25,000 in excess liquid wealth by letting the market do the heavy lifting.

The "Safety Bridge" Concept

When you choose to invest your mortgage overpayments, you aren't just chasing stock market gains; you are building a liquid, secondary emergency fund.

The Trapped Equity Problem: If you aggressively pay an extra $40,000 into your mortgage principal and then lose your job, the bank still expects a mortgage payment next month. You cannot simply 'withdraw' that $40,000 in equity to buy groceries or cover an emergency.

Building the Bridge: By redirecting those same overpayments into a taxable brokerage account instead, you keep your wealth within reach. While equity is 'trapped' inside your drywall, brokerage funds stay liquid. Liquidity is your ultimate defense and the best option for financial flexibility.

Which Path is Right for You?

Choose Early Payoff if: Your rate is 6% or higher, or your ultimate goal is the peace of mind of having no mortgage.

Choose Investing if: Your rate is less than 6% and you have a high-risk tolerance for potentially higher returns while having the financial flexibility of a liquid brokerage account.

Grey Zone Debts: As we discussed back in Chapter 7, debts between 3.5% and 6% fall into the 'Grey Zone.' The same rules apply to your mortgage: the math says invest, but if paying it off gives you more peace of mind, then pay it off. There is no wrong answer. It comes down to personal preference.

Red Flag Financial Behavior: If you find yourself considering an **Ad-**

justable Rate Mortgage (ARM) to "afford" a big purchase, stop and reassess. Avoid these entirely unless you have a guaranteed plan to sell or refinance before the rates jump.

Action Steps

- Assess your rate: If below 6%, calculate potential growth using an investment calculator (e.g., assuming 7-10% returns over 10-20 years).
- Open a brokerage account and invest $100–$500 monthly in a total market or S&P 500 index fund this month.
- Set a timeline: Mark your calendar for a 10-, 15-, or 20-year review to evaluate payoff.
- Track progress: Celebrate milestones, like your fund reaching $20,000, to build momentum.

CHAPTER 15

Leveling Up Your Wealth Building

You've built a solid foundation. You've mastered budgeting, you have an emergency fund, your investing and even looked at increasing your income. Now, it's time to level up with more advanced strategies that fit your working-class reality. We'll keep it simple and practical, while focusing on growing your overall wealth. Let's dive into accessible ways to boost your financial journey, with some examples to show you it's possible.

The Wealth Building Order of Operations

Before executing any of the more advanced strategies in this chapter, confirm that your money is in the mathematically optimal order. Though many of the topics were discussed earlier in the book, for peak efficiency, you need to move from the first bucket to the next without jumping out of order to ensure you don't leave free money or tax breaks on the table.

The Foundation and The Free Money: Save at least 1 month of essential living expenses in a High-Yield Savings Account (actively building toward 3 to 6 months). Also, contribute exactly enough to your employer's 401(k) to obtain 100% of the company match.

Eliminate High-Interest Debt: Eliminate all high-interest consumer debt (except mortgage), using the snowball or avalanche debt payment methods.

The Triple-Tax Weapon: If you have a High Deductible Health Plan, max out your Health Savings Account (HSA). As previously discussed, it goes in tax-free, grows tax-free, and comes out tax-free for medical costs.

Tax-Free Growth: Max out a Roth IRA. You've already paid taxes on this money, so each dollar of growth is yours forever.

The Pre-Tax Max: If you can max out your Roth IRA contributions and have excess to invest, return to your employer 401(k) and increase your contributions up to the annual IRS limit.

The Wealth Multiplier: Only when all prior buckets are filled, and your emergency fund reaches 6 months, should you consider opening a standard taxable brokerage account to invest the overflow.

Maximize Your Retirement Accounts

The Backdoor Roth IRA

If your 2026 Modified Adjusted Gross Income (MAGI) exceeds $168,000 as a single filer, or $252,000 if married filing jointly, the IRS legally bars you from contributing directly to a Roth IRA. But you are not locked out of tax-free growth; you are officially in 'Backdoor Roth' territory. By utilizing an IRS-permitted conversion strategy, high-income earners can still contribute to a Roth IRA. Double-check tools like TurboTax's Roth IRA calculator to confirm your eligibility.

WARNING FOR THE PRO-RATA RULE TRAP

Do NOT attempt a Backdoor Roth conversion if you have ANY existing pre-tax funds in a Traditional IRA, SEP-IRA, or SIMPLE IRA. Under the IRS 'Pro-Rata' rule, you cannot tell the government to convert only your new, after-tax money. The IRS treats all your Traditional IRAs as one giant, mixed bucket. If you mix new after-tax money with old pre-tax money, a massive chunk of your conversion will become immediately taxable.
Tax laws are complex and highly specific to your personal income. **Always consult a certified CPA before executing ANY advanced strategies before attempting it yourself.**

How to Execute It Safely

1. Contribute cash to a non-deductible Traditional IRA.
2. Immediately click 'convert to Roth IRA' inside your brokerage portal before the cash has time to earn interest.
3. File IRS Form 8606 at tax time to prove this was after-tax money.

Since there are no income limits on Traditional IRA contributions or Roth conversions, this move allows high earners to bypass the standard restrictions legally. Just be sure to **file IRS Form 8606 with your taxes** to prove you already paid taxes on that money, ensuring the conversion remains a tax-free event.

Take Advantage of Employee Stock Purchase Plans (If offered)

Think of an Employee Stock Purchase Plan (ESPP) as a coupon for your company's stock. It's one of the few opportunities to buy an asset for less than its current value the moment you acquire it. ESPPs allow you to purchase company stock at a discounted rate, typically 10% to 15% below market price, through easy payroll deductions.

Imagine acquiring shares of your company at a discounted price, sometimes with a "lookback" feature that bases your discount on the lowest price at the start or end of the offering period. Paired with the lookback feature, it's no surprise that most experts see ESPPs as a smart choice: you're essentially earning an immediate return on your investment, provided you sell after buying. The IRS limits contributions to $25,000 per year, but even investing a small percentage of your salary can add up quickly.

The beauty of ESPPs lies in their simplicity and potential. They allow employees to automate savings by allocating a portion of each paycheck, and if the company's stock performs well, the employee could see gains well beyond the discount. Plus, if the employee holds the shares for at least one year after purchase and two years from the start of the offering period, any profit (beyond the discount) may qualify for lower capital gains taxes, further boosting the returns. ESPPs offer a structured way to invest in a company you know well, your own, while leveraging insider confidence in its future.

Maximizing Your ESPP Tax Benefit

To receive the maximum tax benefit from your Employee Stock Purchase Plan, the IRS requires you to meet two specific holding periods simultaneously. If you miss either, you lose the "Qualifying" status and pay more in taxes.

The Two Rules for "Qualifying Sale"

To unlock the lowest possible tax rate on your ESPP profits, you must satisfy both of the following IRS timelines simultaneously:

Rule 1: The 2-Year Clock. You must hold the shares for at least two years from the Offering Date (the day the multi-month enrollment window officially began).

Rule 2: The 1-Year Clock. You must also hold the shares for at least one year from the Purchase Date (the day your payroll cash was actually swapped for company shares).

Sell a day early, and you trigger a 'Disqualifying Sale,' shifting your profits back into your higher ordinary income tax bracket.

Some companies offer 24-month periods, staggered into four 6-month purchase dates. In a long Offering Period example, you might meet the 2-year Offering Date requirement almost the same day you buy the shares. However, you still must wait 1 year from the Purchase Date to satisfy the second part of the rules for a Qualifying Sale. The offering date and purchase dates line up only if your company's plan uses a simple 6-month window with a single purchase. If your plan has a Lookback feature or lasts longer than 6 months, the Offering Date will almost always be 6, 12, or 24 months older than your Purchase Date.

ESPP Qualifying Sale Summary: Buy at a discount, hold for 2 years for less taxes. Selling before the 2-year mark could trigger a higher tax bill.

Hard Numbers Example

Assumptions for 100 Shares:

- Offering Date Price: $100
- Purchase Date Price: $120 (Stock went up during the period)
- Your Discount (15%): You pay $85 per share (15% off the $100 offering price).
- Sale Price: $150 (Stock went up after you bought it)
- Tax Rates: 24% Ordinary Income / 15% Long-Term Capital Gains.

The Result: Waiting for the "Qualifying" period saves you $450 in taxes on every 100 shares in this scenario.

Why the difference?

- **Disqualifying Sale:** You pay your high Ordinary Income tax rate on the entire "bargain element" (the difference between what you paid and the market value on the day you bought it). Any further gain is taxed at short-term capital gains rates (same as your income rate) unless you held it at least 1 year.
- **Qualifying Sale:** The amount taxed as "Ordinary Income" is capped at the original 15% discount. Everything else, even the growth that happened *during* the offering period, is taxed at the much lower Long-Term Capital Gains rate.

The Bottom Line

If you sell immediately (Disqualifying), you pay "income taxes" on the growth that happened while you were saving. If you wait (Qualifying), you shift that growth into the "long-term capital gains" bucket, which is usually taxed at 10–15%.

What To Do If You Are Offered ESPP

To make the most of an ESPP, check your plan's details with your HR department and consider contributing as much as you can if the discount is strong and your company is stable. Many financial advisors suggest selling shares as soon as they meet the qualifying holding period to lock in gains and diversify into other investments, like index funds or bonds, to spread your risk. While ESPPs are a fantastic opportunity, they're not risk-free; investing too much or holding for too long in a single company's stock can backfire if the business struggles. Still, with a smart approach, an ESPP can be a powerful tool to build and accelerate wealth while you work.

Low-Cost, High-Impact Investing

As discussed in Chapter 8, even most Wall Street hedge fund "experts" do not outperform the S&P 500 over 20 years. This supports the strategy of sticking with low-cost, diversified options, such as a broad-market ETF like VTI. These funds spread your money across hundreds of companies, reducing risk while aiming for steady annual returns. However, if you're confident in your knowledge of the stock market and want to take on more risk than a full S&P 500 index fund or ETF, you can consider **sector-specific ETFs** like FTEC, Fidelity's tech-sector ETF that covers the top tech companies on the stock exchange. Other high-performing sector-specific ETFs in recent years include VGT, XLV, VFH, FNCL, and SMH.

Keep in mind**, recent outperformance does not guarantee future results**, as past winners often cycle out of favor. Additionally, sector-specific ETFs are inherently less diversified and tend to experience sharper downturns and higher volatility compared to broad-market benchmarks like VOO. Avoid ETFs that have a high expense ratio of 0.50% or higher altogether as they'll more often than not be a burden to your retirement portfolio. Expense ratios of 0.16%-0.45% are more acceptable in emerging markets, small-cap value, or specialized international funds where the administrative cost of buying the stocks is legitimately higher.

If you're nervous about picking sector-specific investments but also want to explore more than the S&P500, try a robo-advisor like Betterment or Wealthfront. They build portfolios for you, often for fees under 0.25%. You can start with as little as $100. These platforms use the same principles as the pros, diversification and low costs, but make it hands-off for busy folks like you. **Important Note:** The tickers listed in this chapter are examples of the asset class, not specific endorsements. Ensure any allocations across sectors or robo-advisors align with your personal risk tolerance.

Dividend Stock ETFs

If you want to feel like a true partner of a business, dividend stocks can be your best friend. Some established, profitable companies don't just reinvest all their cash into growth; they pay a portion of it directly to you, the shareholder, as a "thank you" for holding their stock. Dividends are not “extra” returns; they're simply one part of a stock's total return, and in taxable accounts they can create ongoing tax drag compared to growth-focused investments. This creates a stream of passive income that hits your account regardless of daily stock prices.

For example, consider a company like Verizon (stock ticker: VZ). They have a history of paying a dividend yield of around 6%. That means for every $1,000 you invest, you can expect to receive about $60 a year just for sitting on the couch. The real "secret sauce," however, is the **Dividend Reinvestment Plan (DRIP)**. You can set your brokerage account to automatically buy more shares of that stock with the dividends you receive. This creates a powerful compounding cycle: your dividends buy more shares, which then pay you even more dividends next quarter. Over a decade, this "snowball effect" can turn a modest investment into substantial wealth without you ever having to lift a finger. In most investing apps like Fidelity or Schwab, setting up a DRIP is as simple as checking the 'Reinvest Dividends' box when you buy the stock.

The Dividend Hierarchy

In the world of investing, consistency is more impressive than size. A company that pays a huge dividend today but cuts it next year is a liability, which is why professional investors group companies into tiers based on how long the companies have successfully raised their payouts. This hierarchy allows you to prioritize the safety of the payment over the headline yield.

Dividend Aristocrats: The 25-Year Standard

A company is crowned a Dividend Aristocrat if it has increased its base dividend every single year for at least 25 consecutive years. Beyond the time requirement, they must also be members of the S&P 500, meaning they are among the largest and most liquid companies in the United States. This 25-year window forces a company to prove it can grow through multiple economic recessions, market crashes, and interest rate spikes without missing a payment. Household names like Johnson & Johnson (JNJ), Procter & Gamble (PG), and Coca-Cola (KO) are the pillars of this group. While you can buy these stocks individually, most investors currently prefer the **ProShares S&P 500 Dividend Aristocrats ETF (NOBL),** which holds all 70+ members for a modest fee.

Dividend Achievers: The 10-Year Proving Ground

The step below the Aristocrats is the **Dividend Achievers, which includes companies that have increased their annual dividend for at least 10 consecutive years**. This group is much larger, often comprising around 400 companies, and includes faster-growing "modern" leaders such as Microsoft (MSFT) and UnitedHealth Group (UNH). Because the entry requirement is only a decade, this tier captures high-performing companies that haven't been around long enough to be Aristocrats but have reached stable profitability. These "Achievers" often offer higher dividend growth rates, meaning they may raise their payouts by 10%

or more each year, whereas Aristocrats tend to provide smaller, steady raises. You can easily own this tier through the **Vanguard Dividend Appreciation ETF (VIG)**, which is known for its ultra-low fees.

Why the Tiers Matter for You

Focusing on these tiers helps you avoid the "yield trap," a stock that looks like it has a huge 10% dividend just because its price is falling due to internal issues. By sticking to Aristocrats and Achievers, you choose companies with a proven track record of prioritizing dividend payouts to shareholders. For maximum stability, go with the **Aristocrats through NOBL**. If you're willing to take more risk and want a combination of income and the chance for the stock price to increase significantly, the **Achievers through VIG** are usually the better option.

Accessible Real Estate Investing Without Breaking the Bank

Real estate ownership can often seem out of reach, but it's not. The easiest way to invest in real estate is through **Real Estate Investment Trusts, a.k.a. ("REITs")**. Through REITs, individuals can invest in large-scale, income producing real estate, such as data centers, commercial medical buildings, and apartment complexes, through a standard brokerage account, completely removing the headache of being a landlord, managing tenants, or fixing repairs. To maximize your REIT investment growth, you should always set your account to automatically reinvest the dividends, using those payouts to buy more shares and harness the full power of compounding.

Unlike private real estate apps or physical property, publicly traded REITs are very liquid—meaning if you encounter an emergency, you can sell your shares and get your cash almost immediately without being stuck by platform lock-up periods.

Individual Stock Picks – Value Investing

If you decide to invest in individual stocks, it must be done strictly with discretionary funds—meaning the "fun money" that is not needed to cover your essential bills, your emergency fund, or your core retirement investments.

The bottom line is that you must learn how to properly evaluate a company's true worth before buying its stock by understanding its **Intrinsic Value**. Intrinsic value is the calculated "true," fundamental worth of a company independent of its current listed market price. It is determined using various valuation models that factor in real financial data, earnings, and assets. If an asset's intrinsic value exceeds its current market price, it is considered undervalued. Value investing was innovated by Benjamin Graham and made famous by his student, Warren Buffett. If it's a good enough system for the best investor in history, it is good enough for you and me.

Rules of Engagement For Stock Picks

Read *Rule #1* by Phil Town for a modern, accessible take on the principles and math. Then, read Chapters 8 and 20 of *The Intelligent Investor* by Benjamin Graham. ***Word of Warning:*** *Graham's entire book tends to read like a dense 1940s textbook. Do not get bogged down in the math; just focus deeply on Chapters 8 and 20 to understand the psychology of the market.* If reading isn't your thing, look up YouTube videos from Phil Town or trusted financial personalities discussing the value investing principles Ben Graham, Warren Buffett, and Phil Town preach. Pay close attention to how Phil Town defines a "moat"—the built-in advantages that protect a business from competitors. All of these teachings will hammer home the "Margin of Safety," which means buying a stock cheap enough that you don't lose your shirt if your calculations are slightly off. Most importantly, these will teach you to ignore the daily ups and downs of the stock ticker; the price of a stock is often driven by temporary panic or hype rather than the company's underlying value.

Protect Your Core: Once you understand the key principles, use a small portion of your discretionary funds to start choosing stocks. Never over-leverage yourself, and never use funds you cannot afford to lose permanently.

Beware of the "Pump-and-Dump": Be fiercely diligent and ignore "get-rich-quick" stock picks from social media influencers. More often than not, they are running illegal pump-and-dump schemes. They get a kickback from a worthless company to push the stock, drive the price up for a day or two, and then sell their shares for a massive profit—pulling the rug out and leaving their followers holding the bag.

Example Breakdown

A simple way to tie all of these strategies together is to think in "buckets" across both your investments *and* your account types.

Potential Portfolio Mix Example

- 60-65% in low-cost, broad-market index funds and ETFs (your core foundation)
- 10–15% in dividend-focused ETFs (like Dividend Aristocrats)
- 10%-15% in individual stocks of 3-5 top tier companies that pass the 4M test taught by Phil Town (Meaning, Moat, Management, and Margin of Safety)
- 5–10% in REITs for real estate exposure
    - Remember to review and rebalance your individual stock picks and grouping percentages yearly.

CHAPTER 16

Financial Independence & Income Streams

Financial Independence (FI) means your investments cover all your expenses, allowing you to live on your terms, whether that involves quitting your current job, or traveling. To find your FI number, multiply your annual costs by 25: for example, $75,000 a year requires $1.875 million invested at a 4% withdrawal rate. It may seem overwhelming, but small steps will help you reach it. These habits will teach you how to save aggressively and diversify income for greater freedom.

Why Financial Independence Matters

Financial independence provides options without financial worries. Without it, you're tied to a paycheck and vulnerable to layoffs or burnout. Aggressive saving and multiple income streams accelerate your FI path, whether you aim for full financial independence or simply more work-life balance.

Avoiding a Fixed Retirement Budget

When you stop earning a salary, your fight against inflation does not stop. If you plan to withdraw a fixed $80,000 every single year of your retirement, you will eventually go broke; twenty years from now, that $80,000 will only buy what $45,000 buys today. You shouldn't have to downgrade your lifestyle every year just to survive.

Instead, calculate your financial independence using the 4% Safe Withdrawal Rate (SWR). This rule allows you to safely withdraw 4% of your total portfolio in your first year of retirement, then adjust that amount upward each subsequent year to keep pace with inflation. The remaining 96% of your portfolio stays invested in the market. By sticking with a balanced, diversified approach, the remaining balance acts as an engine that historically generates enough growth to support your ever-increasing withdrawals for at least 30 years.

You can also adjust this rule based on your timeline: if you are planning for a 40-year retirement, you may want to aim for a more conservative 3.5% withdrawal rate. Conversely, if your retirement will be closer to 15 or 20 years, a 5%, 6%, or potentially 7% SWR may be the right fit.

Stress Testing Your Retirement Plan

A simple retirement planning timeline to remember is the 10-5-2 sequence. When you are about 10 years away from your projected retirement date, you should consult with a fee-only Certified Financial Planner (CFP) to ensure your math holds up. A CFP will stress-test your plan against your specific risk level and goals, ensuring your investments are properly balanced and letting you know if you need to bump up your contributions. Once you confirm your plan is on track, check in with them again at the 5-year mark, and again around the two-year mark (18 to 24 months before your retirement date) to help optimize your final retirement date.

Strategies for Early Financial Independence

Save Aggressively: While saving 10%-15% is the baseline for a traditional retirement, true financial independence often requires more velocity, especially if you didn't start to invest until late 20s or 30s. If this is the case for you, try to aim for 20%-30%, or even 40% if possible, to significantly shave years off your working life. This strategy is part of the FIRE movement and is described in greater detail below.

Invest Wisely: Even though you may be contributing more money each month toward your retirement, it's recommended to continue investing in low-cost index funds or ETFs, as previously covered, to grow your wealth steadily. However, always remember that all investing holds risk, and gains are ***not guaranteed.*** As previously mentioned, you can consider investing in specific sectors with more potential upside. Just remember that the investment opportunities with the greatest upside usually also carry the most risk. If you are pursuing FIRE, your foundation must be rock-solid. Speculative sector bets should never make up more than 5-10% of your total portfolio. Be sure to perform your due diligence before picking any specific fund or stock.

Build a Side Hustle: A $200 a month gig (e.g., tutoring, freelance editing) adds $2,400 in income each year, which grows to $105,000 in 20 years if earning 7% compounding returns.

Real Estate Investment: As we discussed in Chapter 15, Real Estate (specifically REITs) serves as your heavy lifter for diversification. Now that you are chasing Financial Independence, your goal isn't just to 'own' shares—it is to build a 'Rent Replacement' engine.

The Strategy: Shift your REIT dividends from 'Reinvest' to 'Payout' only once you hit your financial independence number. Until then, let the compound interest described in Chapter 7 do the heavy lifting. But what if waiting until you have the full $2 million sounds impossible? Or what if you don't want to retire early, but you want to stress less? That is where **Hybrid FIRE** changes the game.

Understanding the "Hybrid" FIRE Strategies

While standard Financial Independence (FI) focuses on building a massive nest egg to quit working entirely, two popular "hybrid" strategies allow you to reclaim your time much sooner. These are perfect for those who enjoy working but want to leave the high-stress corporate grind.

Coast FIRE: The "Hands-Off" Method

Coast FIRE is the point where you have enough money in your retirement accounts *today* that, even if you never contribute another cent, your investments will grow to support your full retirement by the time you reach age 65.

- **The Logic:** You front-load your savings in your 20s or 30s to take advantage of compound interest. Once you hit your "Coast Number," you stop saving for retirement and only work to cover your current annual living expenses.
- **Simple Calculation (The Easy Way):** Instead of using a complex formula with exponents, use the **"Doubling Rule."**

Historically, invested money tends to double roughly every 10 years (assuming a 7% return). You can work backward from your age 65 goal:

30 Years to Retirement (Age ~35): You need 1/8th of your final goal invested today (It doubles 3 times).

20 Years to Retirement (Age ~45): You need 1/4th of your final goal invested today (It doubles 2 times).

10 Years to Retirement (Age ~55): You need 1/2 of your final goal invested today (It doubles 1 time).

The Math in Action: If you want **$1.5 million** at age 65:

At Age 35, you need roughly **$187,500** invested today ($1.5M ÷ 8).

At Age 45, you need roughly **$375,000** invested today ($1.5M ÷ 4).

At Age 55, you need roughly **$750,000** invested today ($1.5M ÷ 2).

If you have that number in your account right now, congratulations: You are Coast FIRE. You can stop saving for your "Old Self" and spend your income on your life today.

Important Caveat: The Margin of Safety, The "Doubling Rule", and Coast FIRE calculations are based on historical stock market averages, which are never guaranteed. If future market returns fall below historical norms, your portfolio will take much longer to grow. Because of this, it is highly recommended to overshoot your projected Coast FIRE target by 15% to 20% to include a safety margin. Always consult with a Certified Financial Planner (CFP) and/or a CPA to run a personalized projection before you officially stop making retirement contributions.

Barista FIRE: The "Partial Peace" Method

Barista FIRE is for those who have a significant nest egg but aren't quite ready for full retirement. You use a "Safe Withdrawal" from your portfolio to cover a portion of your bills, while a part-time or low-stress job (like being a barista) covers the rest.

- **The Logic:** This strategy often bridges the gap for people who need a job for social interaction or specific benefits, like health insurance, while their investments do the heavy lifting for their mortgage or rent.
- **Simple Calculation:** Required Portfolio = (Annual Expenses - Annual Part-Time Income) X 25
    - *Example:* If you need **$60,000** a year to live, but you earn **$25,000** working at a local shop, your portfolio only needs to provide **$35,000**. Using the 4% rule, you would need **$875,000** invested to be Barista FIRE ($35,000 X 25).

The 3.5% Safety Net Adjustment: The standard 4% rule (multiplying by 25) assumes a traditional 30-year retirement. Because Barista FIRE starts much earlier, your money needs to last longer. For a safer 3.5% withdrawal rate that protects against inflation, multiply your required portfolio withdrawal by **28.5** instead. Always consult a CFP to stress-test your numbers before making the leap.

Which One Fits Your Path?

- **Choose Coast FIRE** if you've saved enough today that your investments will grow to fund your future retirement on their own. You still work to pay your bills now, but you never have to save another penny for the future.

- **Choose Barista FIRE** if you want to leave your high-stress career as quickly as possible. You'll work a part-time job to cover some expenses and withdraw a small, safe amount from your existing investment account to cover the rest of your bills.

Action Step

- **Calculate what your exact Coast FIRE number is by using the 'Doubling Rule' today.**

CHAPTER 17

Giving, Lifelong Learning, & AI: Your Modern Toolkit

Financial freedom is not just about having high account balances; it's about living a life that matters to you. Wealth without purpose can feel hollow. This chapter will show you how to align your new independence with things you value the most in life, whether it is donating to causes you love or mentoring others.

Why Giving and Learning Matter

Giving, whether time or money, builds purpose and community. Donating $20 a month to a cause you care about creates ripple effects. Learning keeps you sharp, helping you avoid mistakes such as overspending or making poor investments. Together, they ensure your wealth serves more than just you.

Giving With Intention Once Financially Secure

How Much: Donate 1–5% of your income to causes like social concerns, education, or health. A $75,000 earner giving 1% of their income donates $750 a year to causes they care most about.

Verify Impact: Use Candid.org or Charity Navigator to check a charity's transparency.

Give Time: Volunteering an hour a month to mentor, coach, or serve at a shelter amplifies your impact.

Using AI to Power Your Financial Journey

Many AI tools are free, always-available guides that can make your path of personal finance easier. No matter what you want to learn, AI can provide quick, personalized answers to boost your progress. This section shows you how to use AI for key steps discussed earlier, with specific prompts to get started today. No technical skills needed, just a smartphone or computer and curiosity. Use these tools to save time, money, and stress on your journey. Avoid using AI for tax codes, contribution limits, or specific investment choices, as training data is often outdated and they are known to make mistakes.

Digital Tools to Start With

These tools are user-friendly, perfect for beginners, and typically offer a free basic version (with optional paid premium features). Access them on your phone or computer to jumpstart your financial journey:

- **ChatGPT**: Ask any financial question or get step-by-step plans (chat.openai.com).

- **Grok**: Get concise, practical answers for budgeting or hustles on their basic app. (Found on X, formerly Twitter).

- **Gemini**: Google's AI model, excellent for researching financial concepts through text and analyzing uploaded documents or images. (gemini.google.com)

- **AInvest**: Free stock research and portfolio tips tailored to your risk level (ainvest.com).

- **Khan Academy** – For fundamentals in economics and personal finance.
- **Coursera / edX** – Free courses from top universities (audit the classes).
- **Podcasts** – Use AI to recommend trusted finance or business podcasts based on your interests.
- **YouTube with AI summaries** – Tools like YouTubeDigest or AI plugins can summarize videos and even suggest what to watch next.

How to Use AI Effectively

- **Be specific**: Ask "How do I save $100 a month on groceries?" instead of "How do I save money?"
- **Verify AI answers**: Cross-check AI suggestions with trusted sources like NerdWallet or Bankrate to avoid misinformation and confusion.
- **Start small**: Try one prompt today, like researching a budgeting app or side hustle idea.
- **Cross-reference**: Use AI to dig deeper into any chapter. For instance, if you are going through Chapter 5, do not ask the AI for live interest rates, as data can lag. Instead, ask: "What are the most reputable websites to check live, updated High-Yield Savings Account (HYSA) rates today?"

AI for Budgeting (Chapter 3)

AI can analyze your spending, recommend budgeting tools, or recommend videos to watch to help keep you on track. Ask AI to break down complex financial concepts or find ways to cut expenses, saving you hours of research.

- "Suggest three free budgeting apps for someone earning $55,000 a year and explain their key features in simple terms."
- "Provide a vetted 5-10 minute YouTube video explaining budgeting in simple terms."

AI for Learning New Skills (Chapter 11)

Upskilling boosts your income, and AI can guide you to free or low-cost resources tailored to your goals. Whether it's mastering Excel or exploring real estate, AI curates trusted content fast.

- "List three free, trusted YouTube videos or courses to learn Excel for beginners, focusing on budgeting skills."
- "Summarize the key points of 'The Simple Path to Wealth' by JL Collins in 300 words or fewer."

AI for Side Hustles (Chapter 11)

Starting a side hustle adds income streams, and AI can help you brainstorm, plan, or scale gigs like tutoring or freelancing. It's like having a coach to refine your ideas.

- "Give me a realistic 30-day plan to start a freelance writing side hustle for under $100, including free tools I can utilize."
- "What are five low-cost side hustles for a retail worker with no experience, and how do I start one within 30 days?"

Why AI Matters

AI cuts through information overload, saving you time and money. A single prompt can replace hours of Googling or expensive courses. For example, asking "How do I start a $150 per month tutoring side hustle?" could lead to $1,800 in extra income per year. In today's fast-moving world, AI is your shortcut to smarter financial decisions.

Action Steps

- **Copy one of the AI prompts above into Gemini or ChatGPT today.**
- **Set up a recurring $10 monthly donation to a local charity you care about.**

Important Disclaimer Regarding AI: AI can be a brilliant (and fun) tool to have at our disposal, but it can sometimes 'hallucinate' (make up facts or provide outdated numbers). Always treat AI's advice as a starting point. Then you can verify the final information or numbers through official websites or with a proven professional, such as a CPA or CFP.

Conclusion

As I previously stated in the intro, most people don't fail to build wealth because they don't earn enough; they fail because they aren't disciplined enough or wait too long to start. None of the concepts or math in the book are revolutionary. Building a solid financial foundation is not about finding some hidden trick; it's about executing proven, math-based systems.

I owe a huge debt to the financial minds who make such information readily available today, whether it's Warren Buffett, JL Collins, Ben Felix, Brian Preston, Phil Town, or Marko from Whiteboard Finance (among others not listed). My goal isn't to reinvent the wheel, but to make the proven methods to financial success available and digestible for everyday people.

If you follow the systems taught in this book, consistently stick to your 33% Housing and 15% Transportation guardrails, and build toward investing 15% of your income for retirement, you're doing what 90% of people aren't currently doing. You're choosing short-term discipline for long-term financial freedom.

As you went through these steps, you may have noticed areas where the math allows for more than one correct answer, like choosing whether to aggressively pay off a 5% mortgage or invest the difference. That is intentional. Personal finance is inherently personal. It's not about strict, confining rules; it's about building a foundation so strong that you earn the right to be flexible. Once you master the core principles, you'll have the security and confidence to make choices that suit your specific life, not just a spreadsheet. You don't need perfection or a large salary. You just need action.

You'll be amazed at how much you can save in just one year. In only a few years, you could be free of high-interest debt. In twenty years, you could achieve the financial freedom that many Americans only dream of. As you advance in your journey and become more financially secure, remember to keep the foundational strategies that got you there in the first place. You can eventually add more advanced strategies, such as real estate investing, while avoiding overleveraging yourself and staying disciplined. But for now, just take the first step.

Track one expense tonight. Set up a $25 automated transfer tomorrow morning. Your financial future is entirely in your hands—now claim it.

The 13-Step Practical Plan to Financial Freedom

These steps are meant to guide you toward financial peace of mind and ultimately financial freedom. Follow Step 1 and proceed through the plan in order. Whether you earn $40,000 or $400,000 a year, the principles stay the same.

A Note on Timing: Progress isn't always straightforward. Some steps, like setting up beneficiaries, are "quick wins" you can finish in one afternoon. Others, such as eliminating debt or building your emergency fund to 4-6 months of expenses, may take months or years of discipline to achieve. Trust the process and keep moving forward.

1. Understand Your Numbers & Spend Less Than You Earn

- **Track It:** List income, expenses, debts, and assets to understand your starting point. Track your spending for 30 days to live within your means, focusing on essential bills first.

- **Having A High Income Does Not Equal Wealth:** If you spend as much as (or more than) you earn, you have no wealth at all.

- **Take Action:** Use trusted apps to build control and prevent debt.

If you need additional support, call 211 or visit NFCC.org to connect with trusted local financial counselors.

2. Set Up a Practical Budget & Hard Guardrails

- **The 60/20/20 Framework:** Adopt a 60/20/20 budget if you're a moderate-income earner (adjust to 70/15/15 if lower income, or 50/30/20 if higher).
    - **60% Essentials:** Automatically deposit into a checking account for rent, utilities, groceries, and insurance.
        - **The Big-Ticket Guardrails:** To ensure this bucket doesn't overflow, your total housing costs must never exceed 33% of your net pay, your entire transportation costs must stay under 15%, and the two combined must never exceed a strict 48% maximum limit.
    - **20% Savings/Retirement:** Automate transfers to a high-yield savings account (HYSA) and retirement accounts.
    - **20% Personal Spending:** Direct to a checking account for guilt-free discretionary spending.
- **Put It on Autopilot:** Use your bank's auto-transfer feature to automate deposits, payments, maintain discipline, and avoid late fees.

3. Save a 1-Month "Starter" Emergency Fund

- **The Target:** Save exactly 1 month of essential expenses (Rent + Food + Utilities).
- **The Rule:** Pause all other investing *except* the employer match to reach this goal aggressively.

- **The Location:** Keep it accessible but separate in a High-Yield Savings Account (HYSA) labeled "Emergency Fund." If you use any of these funds, replenishing this account immediately becomes your number one priority before moving forward.

4. Maximize Your Employer Match

- **"Free Money":** Contribute enough to your company's 401(k) plan to get the full match (e.g., start at 3% and build up if they offer more).

- **The Priority:** ALWAYS keep this match in place as long as your 1-month emergency fund is funded; it is essentially a 100% initial return on your money that beats almost any high-interest debt you may have.

5. Get Core Protection in Place

- **Beneficiaries (Free):** Name beneficiaries on *every* financial account (401(k), checking, savings) to bypass probate. This usually overrides a Will, so check these annually.

- **Term Life Insurance (Low-Cost):** If you have dependents, aim for 12-15x your salary in Term Life Insurance. Skip the expensive whole life policies.

- **Will & Proxy (Low-Cost):** If you have dependents or a partner, get a basic will and a healthcare proxy using a trusted local estate attorney or sites like LegalZoom or Trust & Will.

- **Trusts & Umbrella Policy:** Consider a Revocable Living Trust and Umbrella Insurance Policy if your net worth exceeds $500k in non-retirement assets or if you own real estate. Do these after high-interest debt is gone and your net worth is actively growing.

6. Eliminate High-Interest Debt (>6%)

- **The Attack:** Use the Avalanche or Snowball method to tackle debt above 6% (like credit cards).

- **The Exception:** Primary residence mortgages are exempt from this step; treat them as fixed housing costs for now.

7. Build and Maintain Credit

- **The Basics:** Use secured cards with no yearly fees and pay your bill on time, every month. Start with small purchases, such as gas for your car or groceries.

- **Utilization:** Maximize your credit score by paying your monthly balance in full and keep credit utilization below 15%, never exceeding 30%. Avoid "Buy Now, Pay Later" plan entirely.

8. The Split Strategy (Invest 15% & Finish Your Emergency Fund)

- **The Split Strategy:** Now that high-interest debt is gone, allocate your planned savings between retirement and your growing emergency fund (e.g., 7.5% to retirement, 7.5% to your HYSA).

- **The Setup:** Automate weekly deposits to your emergency fund HYSA and a 401(k) or Roth IRA.
  For your retirement account, use a **Target Date Fund** for a smart, hands-off approach, or build your own portfolio using the **four-bucket strategy** (Large Cap, Standard Growth, Small Cap, International) alongside a bond fund for stability. Use the 120 or 110-Rule for simplicity in determining the percentages of each bucket.

- **The Goal:** Once your HYSA has 6-months' worth of essential living expenses, your emergency fund is done and you can redirect all extra cash towards retirement accounts. If you still have extra cash after maxing out retirement accounts, try to build your emergency fund to 12-months' worth of essential living expenses.

9. Increase Your Income

- **Upskill:** Research one in-demand skill in your profession on LinkedIn Learning or Udemy to earn a raise and more opportunities in your career. Alternatively, look into solid-paying union jobs or trades, if you are unhappy with your current career path.

- **Side Hustles:** Explore freelance platforms like Upwork or use free AI tools/apps to brainstorm low-cost side hustle ideas.

10. Maximize Tax-Advantaged Accounts

- **The "Triple Tax" Superpower (HSA):** If you have a High-Deductible Health Plan, max out your HSA for tax-free contributions, growth, and medical withdrawals.

- **The IRA Choice:** Utilize a Roth IRA for tax-free growth. If you are a high-earner barred from direct contributions, consult a CPA to execute the Backdoor Roth strategy.

- **529 Plans for Kids:** Use a 529 for tax-free educational growth for your children, knowing unused funds (up to $35k as of 2026) can now be rolled into their Roth IRA.

11. Mortgage Payoff & The Safety Bridge

- **The 6% Rule:** If your rate is 6% or higher, focus on early payoff. If your rate is below 6%, focus on investing.

    - **Finances vs. Feelings:** If your mortgage rate is below 6%, but paying it off directly brings you significantly more peace of mind than relying on potentially higher stock market returns, do it. There is no wrong answer when buying peace of mind.

- **The Safety Bridge:** Redirect mortgage overpayments into a liquid brokerage account (invested in a broad-range fund such as VOO or VTI). This creates a secondary emergency fund that grows until it can wipe out your mortgage in a single lump-sum payment.

12. Build and Scale Passive Income Streams

- **Real Estate:** Use Publicly Traded REITs to own fractions of properties and earn rental income without the headache of landlording.

- **Dividends:** Invest in Dividend Aristocrats (NOBL) or Achievers (VIG) to create a snowball of passive cash flow. Reinvest the dividend payouts to create a true compound growth snowball effect.

- **The Endgame:** Reach the "Crossover Point," where your passive income exceeds your living expenses, making work completely optional at that point.

13. Give Back & Live Life With Purpose

- **Give With Intention:** Give when you can to things that matter most to you. Teach kids about money or mentor a colleague. Aim to donate 1–5% of your income to causes you care about, or volunteer your time. Use Charity Navigator to verify the charities or organizations.

Testimonial Page

One Small Favor

Thank you for trusting me with helping you with your financial journey.

If you found value in reading Beyond the Paycheck, could you please take 60 seconds to leave a brief review on Amazon?

Even a sentence or two can help others find this guide.

Thanks!

Resources Glossary

This glossary lists key websites and platforms mentioned in Beyond the Paycheck, empowering readers to manage their financial challenges with confidence. Each resource is paired with its primary use to support your journey toward financial independence.

Ally (ally.com): Offers high-yield savings accounts (HYSA) with competitive interest rates (3–5% APY). Use it to build an emergency fund or save for goals like a new car or a down payment on a home.

AnnualCreditReport.com (annualcreditreport.com): Provides free annual credit reports from the three major bureaus (Equifax, Experian, TransUnion). Use it to check for errors that could lower your credit score.

Bankrate (bankrate.com): A trusted source for comparing high-yield savings account rates, loans, and credit cards. Use to find competitive HYSA rates or research financial statistics, helping you make informed decisions to reach your financial goals.

Betterment (betterment.com): A robo-advisor platform for low-cost, automated investing. Start with as little as $100 to build a diversified portfolio with fees as low as 0.25%.

Candid (candid.org): Assesses nonprofit transparency. Use to verify charities before donating for maximum impact.

Charity Navigator (charitynavigator.org): Evaluates charities for transparency and impact. Use to verify organizations before donating to ensure your contributions are effective.

ChatGPT (chat.openai.com): A free AI tool for answering financial questions or generating plans (e.g., budgeting, side hustles). Always cross-check advice with trusted sources, such as NerdWallet.

Coursera (coursera.org): Offers affordable courses ($50–$200) for up-skilling in fields such as coding and project management—audit free courses to boost income without cost.

Credible (credible.com): Compares personal loan and refinancing rates from multiple lenders in minutes. Use to consolidate high-interest debt or refinance student loans.

Credit Karma (creditkarma.com): A free tool to monitor your credit score and track utilization. Use to maintain a score above 700 for better loan rates.

Edmunds (edmunds.com): Provides car pricing, reviews, and true market value data. Use to ensure fair pricing when buying a certified pre-owned vehicle.

Etsy (etsy.com): A platform for selling digital products or crafts as a side hustle. Start with low-effort gigs like selling templates to earn extra income.

Experian (Experian.com): A company that helps people and businesses check credit scores, manage credit reports, and protect against identity theft.

Fidelity (fidelity.com): Offers low-cost brokerage and retirement accounts (e.g., Roth IRA) with ETFs like FSKAX. Use for investing 10–15% of income for retirement.

Glassdoor (glassdoor.com): Provides salary data and job reviews. Use to research your market value and negotiate a 5–10% higher salary.

Honeydue (honeydue.com): A budgeting app for couples to manage joint finances. Use to align on shared goals like a vacation fund during money dates.

Indeed (indeed.com): A job search platform for finding higher-paying roles. Use to explore opportunities for a 5%+ salary increase.

Kelley Blue Book (kbb.com): Offers car valuation and pricing data. Use to determine fair market value when purchasing a used vehicle to avoid overpaying.

Khan Academy (khanacademy.org): Provides free courses on economics and personal finance. Use to build foundational financial knowledge at no cost, making complex topics accessible and less intimidating for learners new to finance.

LegalZoom (legalzoom.com): Offers affordable will and healthcare proxy services. Use to secure your legacy if you have dependents or assets.

Lemonade (lemonade.com): Provides low-cost renters' insurance (e.g., $15/month). Use to protect belongings without draining your budget.

LinkedIn Learning (linkedin.com/learning): Offers courses on in-demand skills such as data analysis. Use to upskill for a raise or new job.

Modified Adjusted Gross Income (MAGI): Your Adjusted Gross Income (AGI) after adding back deductions like student loan interest or tuition. This number determines your eligibility for tax benefits and retirement contributions, guiding your tax planning and retirement strategies.

Morningstar (morningstar.com): Analyzes investment fees and performance. Use to check ETF expense ratios (aim for < 0.5%) for cost-effective investing.

NerdWallet (nerdwallet.com): Compares credit cards, loans, and financial tools. Use to verify AI advice or find low-fee secured cards.

Policygenius (policygenius.com): Compares auto, home, and term life insurance quotes. Use to save $100–$500/year on policies.

Preply (preply.com): A platform for online tutoring side hustles. Start with $150 per month by teaching skills like language or math.

Realtor.com (realtor.com): Tracks local home prices and market trends. Use to avoid overpaying for a home or research house-hacking options.

SideHustleNation.com (sidehustlenation.com): Offers side hustle ideas and strategies. Use to verify AI-generated hustle plans or explore gigs like freelancing.

SoFi (sofi.com): Provides high-yield savings accounts (3.5–5% APY) and personal loans for debt consolidation. Use for emergency funds or refinancing high-interest debt.

StudentAid.gov (studentaid.gov): Details federal student loan repayment and forgiveness options (e.g., PSLF). Use to explore income-driven plans if you have federal loans.

TaskRabbit (taskrabbit.com): A platform for freelance gigs like furniture assembly or errands. Use to start a low-effort side hustle for $150–$500 per month.

TurboTax (turbotax.intuit.com): Offers a free Roth IRA calculator and tax estimator. Use to check IRA eligibility or estimate your specific tax bracket.

Upwork (upwork.com): A freelancing platform for skills like writing or design. Use to start a side hustle earning $200–$500 per month.

Vanguard (vanguard.com): Offers low-cost brokerage and retirement accounts with ETFs like VTI (0.03% fee). Use for investing in retirement or taxable accounts.

YouTube (youtube.com): A free platform with channels like The Money Guy Show, Marko - WhiteBoard Finance, Dave Ramsey, Rose Han, Money With Katie, and Ramit Sethi offering practical financial advice. Use this resource to learn great personal finance tips such as budgeting, investing, or side hustle tips through engaging and trusted videos.

Zillow (zillow.com): Tracks home prices and rental potential. Use to research duplexes or homes for house-hacking to offset mortgage costs.

Glossary of Terms

4% Withdrawal Rule: A guideline for financial independence, where you withdraw 4% of your investment portfolio annually to cover living expenses without depleting it, assuming a balanced portfolio. Essential for Chapter 16's FI discussion.

24-Hour Rule / 48-Hour Rule: A strategy to pause 24 or 48 hours before making non-essential or large purchases (e.g., over $500 or $5,000) to avoid impulsive spending and align with financial goals. Chapter 2.

401(k): An employer-sponsored retirement plan where employees can contribute pre-tax dollars, reducing taxable income. Funds grow tax-deferred until withdrawal—chapters 8 &10.

529 Plan: A tax-advantaged savings plan designed for education expenses, offering tax-free growth when used for qualified costs like tuition or books—Chapter 14.

Asset Allocation: The distribution of investments across asset classes (e.g., 70% stocks, 20% bonds, 10% small-cap) to balance risk and growth. Critical for Chapter 8's portfolio-building strategies. Chapter 8.

Backdoor Roth IRA: A strategy for high earners to contribute to a Traditional IRA and then convert it to a Roth IRA for tax-free growth, bypassing income limits. Requires attention to tax rules (e.g., the pro rata rule)—Chapter 15.

Behavioral Finance: A field that studies how psychological biases and emotions, such as fear, greed, or overconfidence, influence financial decisions. It explains behaviors such as panic-selling during market dips or overspending due to FOMO, helping individuals recognize and counter these tendencies to make rational financial choices: Intro + Chapter 1.

Budget: A plan allocating income to expenses, savings, and debt repayment, ensuring every dollar supports financial goals. Essential for Chapter 3's budgeting frameworks. Chapter 3.

Capital Gains Tax: A tax on the profit from selling an asset (e.g., stocks, real estate) at a higher price than purchased. Short-term gains (held <1 year) are taxed as ordinary income; long-term gains (held >1 year) have lower rates (e.g., 0–20% in 2026). Relevant for DAF discussions. Chapters 8 &15.**Collision Coverage**: Auto insurance that covers repairs to your vehicle after an accident, recommended for cars valued over $5,000 to avoid out-of-pocket costs. Chapter 6.

Compound Interest: Interest earned on both the initial principal and accumulated interest, enabling exponential growth over time (e.g., $100 per month at 7% grows to $76,000 in 30 years)—Chapter 8.

Concentration Risk: The risk of loss from investing heavily in a single stock, sector, or asset is reduced by diversifying across multiple investments, such as ETFs—Chapter 8.

Credit Score: A numerical measure (300–850) of financial reliability, based on payment history (35%), credit utilization (30%), length of credit history (15%), new credit (10%), and credit mix (10%). Higher scores (700+) unlock better loan rates—Chapter 7.

Credit Utilization: The ratio of credit card balances to credit limits, ideally kept below 30% (e.g., $200 on a $1,000 limit). Lower utilization boosts credit scores—Chapter 7.

Debt Avalanche: A debt repayment strategy prioritizing the highest interest rate debt first to minimize total interest paid, rolling payments to the next debt after payoff—Chapter 7.

Debt Consolidation: Combining multiple debts into a single loan, often at a lower interest rate (e.g., consolidating an 18% credit card to an 8% loan), to simplify payments and save money—Chapter 7.

Debt Snowball: A debt repayment strategy focusing on paying off the smallest balance first for quick wins, then rolling payments to larger debts to build momentum. Chapter 7.

Deduction: An expense subtracted from taxable income, reducing tax liability (e.g., 401(k) contributions). Supports Chapter 10's tax strategies.

Disability Insurance: Insurance that replaces a portion of income (e .g., 60%) if you're unable to work due to illness or injury. Essential for self-employed readers or those in high-risk jobs, as mentioned in Chapter 6.

Diversification: Spreading investments across asset classes (e.g., stocks, bonds, real estate) to reduce risk. Referenced in investing chapters but not explicitly defined. Chapter 8.

Dollar-Cost Averaging: Investing a fixed amount regularly (e.g., $400 per month in an index fund), reducing risk by buying more shares when prices are low and fewer when prices are high. Chapters 4 & 8.

Emergency Fund: A savings reserve (4–6 months of essential expenses) in a high-yield account for unexpected costs like repairs or job loss, preventing reliance on debt. Chapter 5.

Essentials (60/20/20 Framework): The 60% of income allocated to necessities like rent, groceries, utilities, and minimum debt payments in the 60/20/20 budgeting method. Chapter 3.

Employee Stock Purchase Plan (ESPP): A company-run program that allows employees to buy company stock at a discounted price, typically 5-15% below market value, through payroll deductions, often with tax advantages for holding shares for a certain period—Chapter 15.

ETF (Exchange-Traded Fund): A low-cost investment fund traded on stock exchanges, tracking an index (e.g., S&P 500) or sector, offering diversification with fees often below 0.1% (e.g., VTI). Frequently referenced in investing chapters. Chapter 8.

Expense Ratio: The annual fee an investing fund charges to manage your money. While 0.03% is pennies, a 1% fee (or more) is a "slow leak" that can drain thousands from your future wealth.

FHA Loan: A mortgage insured by the Federal Housing Administration, requiring as little as 3.5% down but with higher interest rates and mortgage insurance premiums—Chapter 9.

Financial Independence Number: The savings needed to cover living expenses without working, calculated as annual expenses × 25 (e.g. , $40,000 × 25 = $1 million). Central to Chapter 16's FIRE discussion. Chapter 16.

FIRE Movement: Financial Independence, Retire Early, a strategy emphasizing aggressive saving (50%+ of income) and investing to achieve financial freedom and retire early (e.g., in your 40s). The goal is to reach financial independence decades ahead of traditional timelines, so work becomes optional, not necessary—Chapter 16.

Freedom Fund: A dedicated savings account for financial goals (e.g., debt repayment, travel, home purchase), used to redirect money from cut expenses to build wealth. Chapter 1

Glide Path: An investment strategy that gradually shifts your asset allocation from higher-risk investments (like stocks) to lower-risk investments (like bonds) as you approach a target date, typically retirement. This helps reduce portfolio volatility and preserve capital as you near your financial goal—Chapter 8.

High-Deductible Health Plan (HDHP): A health insurance plan with lower premiums but higher deductibles, qualifying for an HSA, which offers tax-free savings for medical expenses. Chapters 6 & 10.

High-Yield Savings Account: A savings account with higher interest rates (3–5%) than standard accounts, ideal for emergency funds or short-term goals due to growth and accessibility—Chapter 5.

House Hacking: Renting out parts of your home (e.g., rooms or units) to offset mortgage costs, accelerating financial independence, and generating income. It's a creative way to reduce housing costs while building equity, often used by first-time buyers or aspiring investors—Chapter 15.

HSA (Health Savings Account): A tax-advantaged account for those with high-deductible health plans, allowing tax-free contributions (up to $4,400/individual in 2026. Extra $1,000 if you are 55+) and withdrawals for medical expenses. Chapter 10.

Index Fund: A low-cost investment fund tracking a market index (e.g., S&P 500, VTSAX), offering diversification and long-term growth with fees often below 0.1%—Chapter 8.

Inflation Risk: The loss of purchasing power when prices rise (e.g., 3% inflation reduces $1,000 to $970 in value next year), countered by investments outpacing inflation. Chapter 8.

Liability Coverage: Auto insurance that pays for damages or injuries you cause to others in an accident, required in most states and critical for financial protection._Chapter 6.

Lifestyle Creep / Lifestyle Inflation: The tendency to increase spending as income rises, often on non-essential items like luxury goods, larger homes, or frequent dining out, which can hinder savings and financial goals. For example, a $5,000 raise might lead to a new car payment instead of increased investments, trapping individuals in a cycle of higher expenses—Chapter 2.

Liquidity: The ease of converting an asset to cash without significant loss in value. Relevant for emergency funds and real estate investments. Chapter 5.

LLC (Limited Liability Company): A business structure that separates personal and business assets, offering liability protection and tax deductions for expenses like home offices or equipment—Chapter 11.

Market Risk: The potential for investment losses due to economic or market fluctuations (e.g., an 18% S&P 500 drop in 2022), mitigated by diversification and long-term investing—Chapter 8.

Micro-Investing: Investing small amounts (e.g., purchase round-ups or $5 per month) through apps like Acorns, enabling gradual wealth-building with low entry barriers—chapter 4.

Net Income: Income after taxes and deductions, representing the actual money available for spending or saving. Chapter 3.

Net Worth: The difference between your assets (e.g., savings, investments, property) and liabilities (e.g., debts). It's a snapshot of financial health, crucial for tracking progress toward financial independence in Chapter 2.

Passive Income: Income earned with minimal ongoing effort (e.g., dividends from ETFs like SCHD, rental income. Central to Chapters 11 and 16's discussion on side hustles and financial independence.

PMI (Private Mortgage Insurance): Insurance required on mortgages with less than a 20% down payment, protecting lenders if you default—Chapter 9.

Pro-Rata Rule: A tax rule affecting Backdoor Roth IRA conversions, where existing Traditional IRA balances are taxed proportionately if they include deductible contributions, potentially increasing tax liability (e.g ., $10,000 IRA with $2,000 deductible triggers $400 tax at 24%)—Chapter 15.

Rebalancing: Adjusting a portfolio's asset allocation (e.g., 70% stocks/30% bonds) to maintain desired risk levels by selling high-performing assets and buying underperforming ones—Chapter 8.

REIT (Real Estate Investment Trust): A company or fund that owns or finances income-producing real estate, traded like stocks, providing potential dividends and diversification—Chapter 15.

Roth IRA: A retirement account allowing after-tax contributions with tax-free growth and withdrawals, ideal for lower tax brackets—Chapter 8.

S&P 500: A stock market index tracking the performance of 500 major U.S. companies, used as a benchmark for market growth and a basis for index funds like VOO, FXAIX, or SPY—Chapter 8.

SEP-IRA: A retirement account for self-employed individuals or small business owners, allowing pre-tax contributions up to $72,000 (2026 limit), reducing taxable income with tax-deferred growth. Chapter 11.

Side Hustle: A secondary source of income (e.g., tutoring, freelancing, selling products on Etsy) pursued alongside a primary job to boost savings or accelerate financial goals. Chapter 11.

Sinking Fund: A dedicated savings account for specific future expenses (e.g., car tires, yearly subscription fees, excise tax bills), built through regular contributions. Chapter 4.

Target Date Fund: A mutual fund or ETF that automatically adjusts its asset allocation from higher-risk (stocks) to lower-risk (bonds) as the target retirement year approaches, ideal for hands-off investing. Chapter 8.

Tax-Advantaged Account: A financial account (e.g., 401(k), HSA, Roth IRA) offering tax benefits like deductions, tax-free growth, or tax-free withdrawals to encourage saving for retirement, health, or education. Chapter 15.

Tax Bracket: The range of income taxed at a specific rate. Essential for understanding tax-saving strategies. Chapter 15.

Tax Credit: A direct reduction in taxes owed, often more valuable than deductions (e.g., education credits). Chapter 15.

Term Life Insurance: A life insurance policy providing coverage for a specific period (e.g., 20–30 years) at 12x income, protecting dependents without high costs. Chapter 6.

Traditional IRA: A retirement account with pre-tax contributions, reducing taxable income now but taxing withdrawals in retirement, suitable for higher tax brackets. Chapter 15.

Umbrella Policy: Additional liability insurance (e.g., $1M+) protecting against lawsuits, recommended for those with significant assets (e.g., over $500,000). Chapter 6.

Zero-Based Budgeting: A budgeting method where every dollar of income is assigned a purpose (e.g., expenses, savings, debt repayment), leaving no unallocated funds. It could be compared to 60/20/20 for flexibility. Chapter 3.

References & Notes

Introduction

- Paycheck-to-Paycheck Data: LendingClub and PYMNTS.com. (2024). *New Reality Check: The Paycheck-to-Paycheck Report.*

Chapter 1

- Financial Stress: American Psychological Association (APA). (2023). *Stress in America: A Nation Recovering from Collective Trauma.*

Chapter 2

- Buy Now, Pay Later Risks: Consumer Financial Protection Bureau (CFPB). (2022). *Buy Now, Pay Later: Market Trends and Consumer Impacts.*

Chapter 8

- Active vs. Passive Fund Managers: S&P Dow Jones Indices. (2023). *SPIVA U.S. Scorecard* (Showing the underperformance of active fund managers over 15-20 year periods).
- Missing the Best Market Days: J.P. Morgan Asset Management. (2023). *Guide to Retirement / Eye on the Market Report.*

Chapter 9

- Average Wedding Costs: The Knot. (2024). *The Knot Real Weddings Study*.

Chapter 11

- Salary Negotiation: Harvard Law School Program on Negotiation (PON) / Harvard Business School research on the statistical advantages of initiating salary negotiations.
- Side Hustle Data: Forbes Advisor. (2024). *Side Hustle Statistics: How Many Americans Have One?*
- Independent Worker Earnings: MBO Partners. (2024). *State of Independence in America Report*.

Chapter 13

- Couples and Money: Bankrate. (2024). *Money and Relationships Survey* (Detailing financial friction and overspending arguments among couples).

www.ingramcontent.com/pod-product-compliance
Lightning Source LLC
LaVergne TN
LVHW100732061126
851857LV00011B/496
9798995300809